Mindful Leadership

Nikola Plohr

Mindful Leadership

Theoretical Foundations, Self-Leadership, and Practical Implications

Springer

Nikola Plohr
Hamburg, Germany

ISBN 978-3-658-48299-2 ISBN 978-3-658-48300-5 (eBook)
https://doi.org/10.1007/978-3-658-48300-5

Translation from the German language edition: "Warum Achtsamkeit?" by Nikola Plohr, © Der/die Herausgeber bzw. der/die Autor(en), exklusiv lizenziert an Springer Fachmedien Wiesbaden GmbH, ein Teil von Springer Nature 2023. Published by Springer Fachmedien Wiesbaden. All Rights Reserved.

This book is a translation of the original German edition "Warum Achtsamkeit?" by Nikola Plohr, published by Springer Fachmedien Wiesbaden GmbH in 2023. The translation was done with the help of an artificial intelligence machine translation tool. A subsequent human revision was done primarily in terms of content, so that the book will read stylistically differently from a conventional translation. Springer Nature works continuously to further the development of tools for the production of books and on the related technologies to support the authors.

This Springer imprint is published by the registered company Springer Fachmedien Wiesbaden GmbH, part of Springer Nature.
The registered company address is: Abraham-Lincoln-Str. 46, 65189 Wiesbaden, Germany

Preface

This book is dedicated to the question of how mindfulness and leadership can be thought of together and interwoven in practice. In two parts, a diverse range of reflections is developed to trace one's own patterns, but also to design group dynamics and teamwork more consciously.

The process through which the book guides the readers is not only suitable for executives, but for everyone who wants to engage more with themselves and is open to new suggestions in connecting with others. The considerations made here form the basis for mindfulness-based workshop concepts and business coaching that I offer for leaders, teams and companies.

Conversely, this book benefits from all the clients and companies with whom I have already had the privilege to work and to whom I extend my heartfelt thanks. I would also like to thank Marta Mazur for her support.

Nikola Plohr

Contents

Part I
Inner Leadership

In a world of likes and clicks and followers, in a world that constantly creates stages on which we make ourselves dependent on the judgment of others and crave recognition, it almost amounts to a revolution to turn inward. To seek silence. To immerse oneself in oneself. To switch off the outside for a while to be awake for everything, that is going on inside. And to stay there for a while, perhaps even until boredom sets in or the urge to shift all the discomfort inside to the outside or to seek distraction. And then to persist for another moment and to feel that this impulse passes, too. And over time, an inner abundance sets in that no click and no like in this world can replace.

While reading Maja Göpel's "Rethinking Our World," I stumbled upon the term externalization society, which she uses in reference to Stephan Lessenich. It describes the economic-ecological imbalance in which we find ourselves and from which the Western world rids itself by, for example, externalizing its waste or CO_2. "We are not living beyond our means," writes Lessenich, "but beyond those of others."[1] These processes of externalization occur not only on a global, macrological level, but often also on a micrological, very personal level. For example, when superiors externalize their own feelings of inadequacy by conveying a sense of inferiority to their employees.

This form of externalization at the psychological-mental level does indeed lead to a short-term release of tension in the executive's system and the transmission of negative energy, but a long-term balance is not in sight for any of the participants in this way.

On the part of the employees, a feeling of powerlessness and frustration can then become apparent, which is often vented by expressing the frustrating inner life in corridor conversations and behind closed doors. Again, an externalization process that—although understandable—only tightens the spiral of fear, frustration, and pressure and does not contribute to the solution of the original situation.

---

[1] Lessenich, Stefan: The Deluge Next Door, Munich 2016, p. 196, quoted from: Göpel, Maja: Rethinking Our World. An Invitation, Berlin 2020, p. 123.

Even if the corridor conversation provides brief relief and perhaps even a moment of self-righteousness flares up, the inner life is in turmoil, an enemy image hardens, and the doors to productive cooperation close again by a crucial centimeter.

Countless small and large conflicts have already led to teams becoming divided, promising ideas being discarded, and companies failing. A first step in adopting externalization in a meaningful and conscious way is the so-called Free Writing, an exercise that serves self-reflection, helps to recognize inner patterns and resistances, and to free oneself from burdens without having to burden the environment with unfiltered moods and confusions.Practice: Free Writing

All you require is pen and a piece of paper, because this type of writing works best when, very old school, it is written by hand and not on digital devices. Let the words flow from the body into the hand onto the paper, do not lift the pen, do not pay attention to grammar or sentence structure, do not think about what you are writing, but let everything that you think, that comes up, that pops up, flow out of you. Externalize your thoughts, fragments of thoughts—there is only one rule: Do not lift the pen, do not take breaks, do not think, but really let it flow. Out with it. Yes, with everything. I have often used free writing in workshops and seminars. It is always surprising what happens when heads bow and the participants start writing. After a certain time, often such a deep calm and relief set in that I can even feel them in Zoom workshops. Afterwards I get feedback like: Ah, that felt good. The time was too short. What? That was a whole five minutes? Can we do that again?

This exercise is effective on many levels. Firstly, it provides the space and time to use emerging words to free oneself from the inner tangle of thoughts and topics that we all carry around with us. Secondly, the externalization of the inner life allows for a distancing from it, a re-reading of what is currently happening inside. The continuous self-talk that takes place in all of us, but is often conducted unconsciously, translates into the mediality of writing. Inner patterns can be recognized in this process, as we often unconsciously circulate around the same topics and processes. Free Writing is a wonderful technique to make the subconscious conscious, perhaps even to be able to laugh about the paths that the brain sometimes takes out of sheer habit.

Thirdly, these patterns and thought loops often reveal deeply ingrained assumptions about the world and oneself. For example, one workshop participant was visibly shocked at how often she had written within the five minutes that she was not doing enough, that she had to try harder, that it was all not enough. The participant appeared incredibly disciplined and diligent, but to her inner voice, her inner driver, it never seemed to be enough.

In an in-depth coaching session, we delved into her insights from the Free Writing and investigated the origins of the Not-Enough-Feeling. The results are not always so profound, but it is worthwhile, one way or another, to accept the inner voice, to listen to it, to externalize it, and to be brave enough to read in it.

I often recommend this exercise to teams, especially before difficult or conflict-ridden meetings or even in the middle of them, when discussions become hardened, but no solution is in sight and it feels like all team members keep taking on the same roles again and again. My tip: Press the stop button for a moment, dig out pens and paper and start writing.

If you want to incorporate the practice into your daily routine, I recommend doing it either in the morning or in the evening, and above all, regularly. Those who tend to swap sleep for brooding are warmly invited to try out free writing before going to bed. If the practice is to serve more as a self-reflection tool, then I recommend picking up the pen first thing in the morning.

Introduction—From Inside to Outside

When the term "Mindful Leadership" first popped into my head, I felt like I had discovered a treasure. My whole body tingled, which is always a very good sign for creative processes, and I immediately grabbed a pen and noted down the term. The first disappointment was huge when I researched and noticed: others were faster than me. And at the same time, I had to smile, as my impulse was a sign that my ego was playing a trick on me and turning the "others" into opponents, the found objects into losses of my own ideas, and the creative search for new approaches to leadership into a competition. Wasn't this small process within me already a sign that the topic was far from being exhausted, far from being embodied, far from being fully thought out and written about? Wasn't I myself the best example that a book on this topic could be worthwhile?

Initial conversations with friends, colleagues, but also with clients from individual coaching sessions quickly showed me: Most companies and institutions are still far from concrete practices of mindfulness in corporate environments, from Mindful Leadership as a concept, as a reflection, as an approach. With this book, I want to provide suggestions on how leadership can be rethought and translated into practice under the concept of mindfulness.

The book consists of two parts and first addresses the topic of "Inner Leadership" and then "Mindful Leadership". Two basic assumptions accompany the design of the entire project. *Firstly*, I assume that every person is a *leader*. We all lead a life and ourselves through it. We navigate, make decisions, conduct inner dialogues, have inner teams that we carry around with us and in which a whole variety of opinions and criticisms are exchanged. The question "How do I want to lead my life?" is closely intertwined with the question "How do I want to lead myself in this life?" How can I, for example, motivate myself to make changes, develop new habits, how do I deal with my resources, what kind of narratives do I spin about myself and others in my head, how much do I demand of myself, how much respect do I pay to my own capacities and abilities? How do I

N. Plohr, *Mindful Leadership*, https://doi.org/10.1007/978-3-658-48300-5_1

encounter my inner critics? These and other questions are raised in the first part *Inner Leadership*, framed scientifically and classified into larger subject areas.

The *second* basic assumption that this book follows is as straightforwardly formulated as the first: The way we lead ourselves is the way we lead others.

Following the core of the sentence, the second part of this book is dedicated to the step towards others, into teamwork, and at the same time refers to the insights from the reflections on the topic of Inner Leadership, which comes into focus in the first part.

To bring theory and practice into a balanced relationship and to make the invitation to reflection concrete, this book interweaves literary references and theoretical frameworks with excerpts from interviews and observations from coaching and workshops with executives and teams. In addition, I offer reflection exercises and questions that can not only be tested alone, but also in a team and can serve as starting points for concrete changes.

I write this book at the intersection of science and practice, I write it as an entrepreneur, coach, sociologist, and mix methods and narratives with observations and practices to show ways from thinking to doing. This book is also a result of my own experiences and challenges that I have been and continue to be confronted with in the university context. As a lecturer, I regularly stand in the seminar room and ask myself: How can I encourage students to believe in themselves, to share their abilities, to think independently, to develop their own projects? How can I hold space for diversity, for ambivalence, for doubts and questions but above all for this infinite potential that every group possesses? How can I be a Mindful Leader, as a professor, as a consultant, in my coachings and trainings, and also for my life?

At the beginning of this scientific-practical compilation of approaches is therefore a very personal question, a reflection and research on the responsibility towards my students, clients, my environment and last but not least myself.

With this book, I do not present ready-made answers and certainly no results carved in stone. Instead, I would like to invite you to be curious with me and to explore how we want to think and practice leadership in the future and what we can do here and now, regardless of the position we currently hold. The two terms Inner Leadership and Mindful Leadership hold the space for diverse reflections and approaches, which hopefully will not only find their place in theory, but will also make their way into offices, companies, and personal conversations.

Mindfulness

The term mindfulness is now used in a variety of contexts. It involves a conglomerate of practices, integrates a wide range of programs, such as that of Jon Kabat Zinn[1] and has long been deeply intertwined with one name before its trend-oriented use in guides[2], corporate contexts, and -coachings: Thich Nath Nanh. The Buddhist monk, who among other things established a so-called Sangha, a mindfulness and meditation center in southern France under the name "Plum Village", was nominated for the Nobel Peace Prize after he fought side by side with Martin Luther King for the end of apartheid. A struggle that expressed itself among other things in slow walking meditations, step by step, mindful, slowing movements in the midst of a demonstrating and angry crowd. Each step a breath, each step a pause, a demonstration of senseless violence.

Mindfulness creates space and time, indeed it expands time where it seems to be lacking, where it runs and slips away and sometimes seemingly leaves no space for conscious decisions, conscious encounters, let alone conscious breaths. That's why at its core, mindfulness still contains a moment of resistance.

Mindfulness can be understood as a conscious turning towards the present and what is present here and now. This now and here describes not only the external circumstances, but also our inner life. When we turn mindfully, consciously to our inner selves, we enable ourselves to feel how we (really) are, what patterns are running within us and how we can make the best decisions for ourselves and others from moment to moment. Mindfulness simply allows us to get to know

[1] See, among others: Kabat-Zinn, Jon: Healthy through Meditation, Munich 2013.

[2] Among others: Michael Carroll: The Mindful Leader, Colorado 2007, Gonzalez, Maria: Mindful Leadership. The 9 ways to self awareness, transforming yourself and inspiring others, Ontario, 2012, Janice Marturano: Mindful Leadership. A path to mindful leadership competence, Freiburg 2015, Esther and Johannes Narbeshuber: Mindful Leader. How we take leadership for our life into our own hands and how serenity leads us to success, Munich 2019, Lorelei Kopp: Mindful Leadership: Tools and methods for mindful leadership in turbulent times, Graz 2021.

N. Plohr, *Mindful Leadership*, https://doi.org/10.1007/978-3-658-48300-5_2

ourselves better and thus to explore how we lead ourselves, lead others, lead our lives and how we want and can change it. Inwardly directed mindfulness is anything but egocentrism. It is rather the space in which self-responsibility and self-reflection set in. Moreover, the practice of mindfulness implies that we feel more connected with ourselves, with others and everything that surrounds us.

In "The miracle of mindfulness" Thich Nath Hanh writes as an introductory reading instruction "[…] from now on I'll use the term mindfulness to refer to keeping one's consciousness alive to the present reality."[3]

To maintain a lively, awake consciousness, to perceive the present and to be present at all: all this can be understood as mindfulness. The quoted passage contains an active moment. Keeping consciousness alive and aligning it with the present moment is a practice, an exercise. Thich Nath Hanh formulates at another point in the book: "[…] the presence of mindfulness means the presence of life."[4] Mindfulness means the presence of life.

Life is always present, only our attention often is not. Instead of directing our senses and thoughts to the present moment, we let them scatter and either revolve around the past or construct a future. Without wanting to fall into cultural pessimism, it can be observed that we tend to let ourselves be torn out of our presentness again and again, especially through digital media such as the smartphone, social networks and messaging services. In my workshops on the topic of focus and concentration, the smartphone is always named as the main source of distraction.

From a media science perspective, the smartphone occupies a special position because it combines so many other forms of media. When the smartphone is switched on, users* are addressable and reachable on so many channels at the same time that every vibration, every signal tone can mean anything: From the insignificant Ikea advertisement to the new professional project to the alarming call from the kindergarten. Our nervous systems are therefore constantly ready to react to a potential call and the state of excitement of our bodies and senses is continuously high. It could be something important. And the hand reaches for the smartphone because of the potentiality of an as yet uncertain event, while the current event of the present experiences less attention. Even if we are not aware of it most of the time: This kind of distraction of our concentration, the loss or at least the passing by of the present moment exhausts us. Digital media play a shaping role in this context.[5]

What does mindfulness have to do with mental exhaustion and digital distraction? Thich Nath Hanh writes: "Mindfulness is the miracle by which we master and restore ourselves."[6] The monk is anything but a hermit detached from the world, who retreats to his meditation cushion and turns his back on the world.

---

[3] Thich Nath Hanh: The miracle of Mindfulness, Rider 2008, p. 11.

[4] Ibid. p. 15.

[5] The Vocer Institute in Hamburg researches these connections and focuses on the concept of "Digital Resilience". https://digitale-resilienz.org/#digitale-resilienz, last accessed: 19.12.2022.

[6] Thich Nath Hanh: The miracle of Mindfulness, Rider 2008, p. 14.

He speaks a lot about the topics of burnout and depression in his *Dharma Talks,* which are made directly accessible via Youtube from Plum Village.[7] Many people seek out the Sangha when they feel exhausted and have lost contact with themselves and their (social) environment, or when they feel they need a break, they need recovery. He repeatedly emphasizes that mindfulness and techniques such as conscious, slow walking can help to reestablish contact with nature, with the earth, with one's own body, and gradually to arrive more mentally in the present.

The miracle of mindfulness, which helps us to regenerate and master our lives, is primarily based on the change in perception of the present. It is not necessary (always) for the external circumstances to change in order to experience moments of presence and inner peace. Rather, it is the mindful and present attitude towards these circumstances, a training of the mind, the body, the thoughts and patterns, that makes a different experience possible. The miracle thus lies in an inner change, in a consciousness oriented towards the present and a gentle redirection of one's own perception away from all distractions and scattering towards what is right now. This does not mean, however, that all external circumstances can be made bearable solely through a sufficient degree of mindfulness or that mindfulness suppresses or overlays change processes. In line with the motto: No matter what, if you are mindful enough, everything is fine and nothing has to change externally. Rather, a conscious bundling of attention for the present moment creates space, creates time, and allows clarity for the changes that are really meaningful and implementable. Because, where does change begin? Where do restructuring processes of companies, relationships, life paths begin? Always here and now. So there is no way around the present anyway, and instead of fleeing from it, instead of seeking distractions and scattering, the beginning of the transforming power of the present lies in turning towards it.

With this, I am already in the midst of reflecting on mindfulness practices and approaches for the journey inward and towards what I would like to call "Inner Leadership". Because whatever is going on inside us, to become clear about who we can and want to be and also how we want to lead ourselves and others in this life, we must take heart and turn to this inner self. The miracle of mindfulness can unfold in a special way, especially in times when the belief prevails that we never have time. Because if we manage to fully engage with the present, then TIME IS. Then there is vitality around us and in us anyway and then creativity and flow and connection can arise from this inner vitality. But first, it is important to surrender to the present. The present within, as well as the present outside.

Thich Nath Hanh demonstrates this using the wonderful example of dishwashing. A practice that he initially finds anything but wonderful. But the doing teaches him to give himself to the moment, to fully devote himself to the dishes and to feel the vitality of the present in it. The activity is not aimed at a future purpose, but it is about washing the dishes to wash the dishes: "[...]washing the dishes to wash

---

[7] I delve deeper into the connections between burnout (prevention), mindfulness, and attention in chapter 2.16 "Flow".

the dishes".[8] The devotion to the self-purpose of doing, of the moment, and not the longing for the end of the task is the starting point of happiness and fulfillment. The dishes, but above all his devotion to the moment, bring him into the present, give him the experience of the present, and let him arrive in it.

If we want to find out how we can lead ourselves and our lives, if we want to experience what kind of Inner Leadership we can cultivate, then it is helpful to be mindful, present, and in the present. To really engage with what is inside of us. Mindfulness holds the space for reflection, for a closer look, for conscious decisions, and for an empathy-based coexistence. We don't have to be Zen Buddhist, dishwashing monks to have this experience. It is available at any moment.

To make these theoretical considerations very practical and to make mindfulness experienceable in an equally effective and simple way, I invite you to try the following exercise, which can be wonderfully performed alone or in a team.

In this, we literally follow the traces of Buddhist mindfulness teaching and turn in a new way to an everyday practice that—if we once consider how laboriously we learn it—is actually always a miracle.

Practice: Mindful Walking

Often, all our energy is caught up in our minds. Long periods of sitting, computer activities, and mental work that demands our brain, but less so our whole body, bring their own dynamics. Never in the history of mankind have we moved so little (at least in the western industrial nations) and yet are so advanced on many levels as never before. People run many kilometers on treadmills in fitness studios, but rarely enjoy sticking their noses into the cold, damp November air that is currently wafting towards me from a crack in my kitchen window. We often do not walk to enjoy the walk, but to record the ten thousand steps on our left wrist, to listen to podcasts, to make phone calls, or to run away from the present and unpleasant thoughts. I do not exclude myself from this, often rushing from A to B, equipped with headphones in search of regeneration in nature… which I sometimes deprive myself of when I stare at my smartphone every two meters to check if the world is still there, if someone is addressing me or needs me, or what the weather will be like in ten minutes.

Mindful walking consciously directs attention to the feet and to the contact of the feet with the ground, with the earth. The practice of mindful walking is a technique to reduce stress and to preventively counteract it, to arrive in our body and to connect with our breath. To connect with the earth, our planet, and for all those for whom this seems to much: to connect with the soles of our feet.

If possible, practice outdoors. If you are walking with a group, engage in silent walking and only share your experiences afterwards, if at all. It can also be very powerful to share the experience without translating it into words.

Breathe in, deeply, and take a step. Breathe out, long, and take a step. Continue with this breath-step pace. You will quickly notice that this rhythm greatly slows

---

[8] Thich Nath Hanh: The miracle of Mindfulness, Rider 2008, p. 11.

down your walking. Perhaps it makes you restless at first and the impulse to walk faster arises within you. Calm this impulse by focusing entirely on your steps, your breath, and the harmony of the two. Feel how the heel touches down, how your foot rolls, feel how the air flows in through your nostrils, your chest expands, then flows out again as your foot reconnects with the earth, the ground beneath you. Feel the contact of your sole with the ground, bring your mindfulness into your feet, yes, breathe into your feet. For all non-yoga-experienced, this may sound strange at first, but try it out, the body usually finds this much easier than the cognitive imagination.

Over time, you will notice how steps and breath engage with each other and not only your body, but also your mind calms down. Perhaps you will notice that your senses are sharpened for the many details of your surroundings. For the colors of the leaves, the graininess of the path, small branches and stones. Perhaps something childlike, something awe-inspiring begins to spread within you, if so, let it happen, try not to intellectualize it. If restlessness, frustration, and annoyance spread, let it happen too, but keep walking. Do not hold on to your emotions, but let them go, step by step, breath by breath.

Like so many practices and habits, this one also needs a little time. If you don't like it right away, give mindful walking at least one more chance. And then another. And maybe another. I once heard from a world traveler that only after two thousand kilometers of walking through the Australian Outback did silence set in his head. So don't be too hard on yourself if the experiment in the city park doesn't go quite as zen-like as you imagined it the first time. It still brings you, with every step, more into the present. And that is somehow always the beginning of everything.

Criticism

Aristotle already stated: “There is only one way to avoid criticism: do nothing, say nothing, be nothing.”[1] We are all constantly confronted with criticism, sometimes in a loud, offensive way, sometimes in quiet undertones, sometimes by people close to us, sometimes by strangers whose paths we cross by chance. However, one of the loudest and often most critical voices is the one, we carry within ourselves. We all know them, the inner critics who scold us, who turn our doubts into accusations, our fears into shame and guilt—often we judge ourselves more harshly than we would ever do with good friends.

Often, old fears hide behind our inner criticism and harshness. Like the fear of not being loved, the fear of not being enough, or the fear of failure. Many of these fears culminate in the deep, often existential fear of being excluded.

What the introductory quote from Aristotle also makes clear is that criticism can hardly be avoided, even if we would often prefer to do so. At least when we ourselves are under criticism. In a world of like-economy, where the number of followers and other parameters of quantified attention can quickly be confused with self-worth, sometimes even the like not given feels like criticism.

So how do we find a constructive attitude towards criticism? What definitions and theoretical approaches to criticism can be inspiring in this regard? And how can criticism—both internal and external—be integrated in a meaningful way? The French philosopher and sociologist Michel Foucault defines criticism as “the art of not being governed in such a way.”[2] From this quote, the following points can be derived. First: Criticism is an art that requires attention and practice to master. If we avoid it, we will never learn this skill. Second: Criticism allows us to say no to authorities and actions. This no is not absolute, but integrates a movement towards something else. Criticism does not mean, according to Foucault, *not being*

---

[1] Cited from: Endriss, Lilo: Roadmap for the Flow, Wiesbanden 2019, p. 194.

[2] Foucault, Michel: What is Criticism? Berlin 1992, p. 12.

N. Plohr, *Mindful Leadership*, https://doi.org/10.1007/978-3-658-48300-5_3

governed at all, but not in such a way, not like this, not in this way. This contains the longing to be able to take other, new paths, to behave differently, to think differently. When we deal with our inner critics, we can identify these moments of longing and follow their traces.

In Foucault's quote about the art of not being governed in such a way, there is a moment of reflection for what I call Inner Leadership. Because regardless of external governments, superiors and other authorities, something also "governs" within us. You can call it consciousness or mind or personality, maybe even soul. Beyond the designation, it quickly reveals: We all have such an inner center that controls us, governs us, speaks to us, navigates, decides, steers. If we now practice inner criticism, we learn to differentiate better which voices from our childhood, the immediate environment sound, which beliefs and ideas guide and steer us and whether we actually want to *be governed in such a way*. Or maybe quite differently?

The first step towards a new attitude towards the inner critical voices is to listen carefully and explore them. Often we have been carrying them around with us for so long that we believe them unconditionally or don't even notice anymore that we are continuously exposing ourselves to their criticism.

This was the case with a workshop participant, whom I will simply call Tina for simplicity's sake. Tina runs a consulting firm and leads a team of three employees. The workshop was about time and break management and I combined self-reflection techniques with exercises and group exchange for better communication processes in the team. In the first part, I had the women write down which positive or negative sentences regarding taking breaks came to their minds. There were sentences like "He who rests, rusts" or "Work first, then pleasure". Most Germans probably know these sentences all too well and one can say that they have entered our cultural memory over generations. If we repeat these sentences, pass them on to the next generation, we not only feed the communicative memory of our time, but also prepare the ground for the next and perhaps even the next generation. In times of increasing exhaustion diseases such as burnout, anxiety disorders and depression, it may be time to question the old sentences for their meaningfulness and effect and to replace them with other, more positive formulations.

Back to Tina. In addition to the sentences mentioned above, she also had written: "If I don't work, I'm lazy." I asked her if she might know this sentence from her family history, if she could remember a situation where someone had accused her of being lazy. She quickly dismissed it and said, "No, no, no, that's me, that comes from me. I just always want to accomplish a lot, I get bored quickly, I just like to do a lot." I let it stand and continued the workshop. At a completely different point at a later time, Tina mentioned out of context in a subordinate clause… "oh for my father I don't *really* work. Recently he visited and saw me sitting on the sofa with the laptop and he said, oh so that's how you work, comfortably on the couch, lounging there, sweatpants on-we didn't have that." I looked at her, she looked at me, she let out an "ohhhhh—caught!" and we both had to laugh. The connection had not been clear to her until that moment, even though it seemed so obvious from the outside. This little anecdote contains another insight about our inner critics. If they are internalized voices of our parents, which we repeat over and over again, it is often difficult for us to create distance from them. This contains the deep (childlike!) conviction that if we turn away from our parents' criticism, we are actually turning away from them. As a result, we integrate our parents' criticism as our seemingly self-chosen attitude (Tina: "…I just like to do a lot"). Implicitly, we defend our safety net, our parents, who provide us with protection in childhood. Giving up their criticism feels, paradoxically as it may seem, like giving up their protection.

Of course, it's not always just parents whose criticism we have integrated and repeat. Teachers, professors, superiors, partners—they can all hide behind the supposedly self-critical voices. So it's worth taking a closer look and asking in a second step: Do I want to carry these sentences around with me any longer or is it perhaps time to practice new thought patterns?

We often pass on the voices of our inner critics unconsciously. Parents sometimes tell me that they suddenly utter the very sentences they never wanted to hear again to their children. This can also happen in work contexts when the employee works his way up to the boss and swears to approach everything differently and more relaxed—and then catches himself overwhelmed and shouting in the office.

These repetition loops are human, but they also invite us to deal with them more closely in order to better classify and possibly adjust them. If we do not deal with the way we criticize ourselves, we may externalize the inner critics to free ourselves from them. Brené Brown puts it so nicely when she says: "When I'm scared, I am getting scary."[3] Often people who are overly critical with others are even more critical with themselves. This does not justify it when you come into their focus and get the feeling that you can never please them. But perhaps it allows a little more empathy for these behaviors—because most of the time, overly critical people can please themselves the least.

To trace the paths of the inner critics and learn more about them, the following reflection questions and exercises can be helpful.

1. The already introduced Free Writing is a good technique to externalize and reflect the inner voice, including the critical one. Are there sentences that you keep writing down, that repeat themselves? Who would you attribute them to? A family member? A friend, a partner? A colleague? How old were you when you first consciously heard the sentence? This information is important because we sometimes tend to react from this age—these are the moments when the 42-year-old suddenly stomps, cries, or hides like a five-year-old. Only when we know which part of our inner child[4] we can contact to heal the experience, can we redirect our reactivity.

---

[3] Podcast: Dare to Lead by Brené Brown: Episode Brené with Simon Sinek on Developing an Infinite Mindset, 18.01.2021, last accessed: 28.06.2022.

[4] Stahl, Stefanie: The child in you must find a home, Munich 2015.

2. If a sentence stands out particularly and repeats itself: Look at it very closely. Perhaps it also stems from your own inner criticism. Can you remember a specific situation when it first came to mind? Can you rephrase it positively or take away its potentially hurtful power? If you look at it soberly: Do you really believe this sentence? In Tina's case, we replaced: "If I don't work, I'm lazy" with "I really enjoy doing nothing at all." At the beginning, the first sentence might still often shoot through your head—but the more often you use the other one, the more you can relax into the new pattern. It sometimes also helps to write the new sentence on a post-it and place it within sight. This way, you continuously *re-mind* yourself of your new inner alignment. This process of rephrasing old beliefs is called *reframing* in coaching. You give an old pattern a different frame with a new sentence. The situation remains the same, but you give yourself new reaction possibilities through the power of words.
3. How does the inner criticism manifest physically in you? Do you get warm, do your hands sweat, does your face turn red, does your forehead tighten? Does your stomach react? If there is a physical reaction, first turn to this level and take a deep breath. Direct your attention to the part of your body that reacts and breathe deeply.
4. Is there something constructive in the criticism, an unfulfilled longing or a desire for behavior change that you can read out of the words and use for yourself?
5. Observe yourself honestly to see if you have a tendency to project your inner critical voice onto others, perhaps even to deflect it in order to free yourself from it.

In tracing the paths of the inner critics, not only our attitude towards ourselves often changes, but also towards the people in our environment. The inner exploration of critical voices ideally leads to us striking more conscious and differentiated tones towards others. Especially in work contexts, an open culture of conversation is of immense importance. This also includes constructive criticism.

If all team members are familiar with their inner critics, a good prerequisite is created to engage in conversation without carrying old patterns of reactivity into every meeting. In teams that trust each other, it is also possible to talk openly about one's own patterns. I have already been able to experience and accompany this in several workshops.

For example, at a team morning that was actually about strategies for promoting concentration, it turned out that all four team members had a very strong inner critic who made it difficult for them to take breaks. Each team member was afraid of not accomplishing enough and felt guilty towards the others, who in turn worked more and more because they carried a similar tendency in a voice within them that did not allow them to take a break and said something like: "You are doing too little, the others are much more diligent than you, make sure you can keep up." This spiral had been tightening for months and even led to a woman feeling guilty while having dinner with her husband and answering emails on the side.

When these all too similar experiences and inner voices were shared in the workshop, loud, liberating laughter broke out: Each of the women had projected the inner critic onto the other and the patterns were so similar that they reinforced each other. We used the time of the workshop to establish a clear weekly structure in which work and break times were better regulated and also integrated the "Feel like taking a break?" email, which was to circulate in the team from now on as desired. So now, instead of pressure and critical projections, little reminders for the break from home office to home office flutter around.

Once we have confronted our inner critics and also searched for internal patterns within the team, the question arises as to how we can criticize each other in a meaningful and constructive way, without hurting anyone, but with all the courage for clarity. Interestingly, a few good pointers for the art of criticism did not come to me in books, nor in workshops, but in my yoga teacher training.

In one unit, we talked about the "four gates of speech", which are expressed in the following four questions:

1. **Is it true?** In terms of criticism, it is worth pausing for a moment and asking oneself: Is it a projection of my inner critics onto the other person, or is it something that I really notice about the other person time and again? Does my criticism stem from a flaring emotion or from calm, clear observation? Is the criticism I want to express truthful?
2. **Is it necessary?** Am I really following a necessity when I express the criticism? Is it something that I have been observing for a long time and that does not change by itself? What is the goal of my criticism? Where does the necessity to share my criticism come from?
3. **Is it timely?** Is the person I want to criticize even ready and open to listen to me? Or are they already under constant stress? Do we both have time to talk calmly? Often it is helpful to weigh the necessity and the timing against each other. Criticism is a process—often we carry our points of criticism around with us for a long time, had time to deal with them in detail. The person we may want to criticize may be taken by surprise or confronted with our concern for the first time. Sometimes it helps to spread the timing of the criticism and to arrange at least one more conversation so that what has been said can be processed and reflected upon in the meantime. Often we want to "tick off" criticism because it is uncomfortable to expose ourselves to criticism. But actually, a development often begins with the first mention, which often needs and may take time.
4. **Is it kind?** Can I find constructive and empathetic, but also clear words to formulate my criticism? What is the intention of my criticism? Do I perhaps even see that the person themselves suffers from their behavior? Is there a higher purpose, perhaps even a common goal, that is more within reach by openly expressing criticism? Can I possibly even offer the person help or ask: what do you need from me to change xyz? I would rather ask this last question in a follow-up conversation, once some time has passed to process the points of criticism mentioned.

In this chapter, I have mainly devoted myself to the inner critics, as well as to criticizing each other. Michel Foucault, in his confrontation with criticism as an *art of not being governed so much*, went far beyond this sphere of influence. But ultimately, the great criticism that we may formulate about overarching systems also begins within ourselves. Often in workshops, I have experienced people complaining about "the superiors", but the criticism remained enclosed in their own offices and echo chambers. It takes courage to set out, to present one's concerns and to openly criticize. The *four gates of speech* can serve as preparation. If we believe Aristotle, then criticism cannot be avoided. If we want to be visible and effective in any way, we always expose ourselves to critical voices. Instead of avoiding criticism, holding it back or pouring it unreflectively over others and ourselves, we can face it and recognize its added value. Criticism shows us our limits, but also our integrity, it lets us learn new things about ourselves and others, it prepares the ground for change and growth. One thing is certain: We are all afraid of being criticized. And yet we long to learn an empathetic and constructive way of dealing with criticism. This chapter is an invitation to embark on the journey inward and to listen anew to the critics within us. They have a lot to tell us about ourselves.

Self-Narratives

As a child, I always wanted to become a storyteller. I practiced early on, wrote small texts, wrote long before I could really write, and then invented different stories for the audience depending on the scribbles that filled my books, with which I tried to imitate my mother's handwriting.

Decades later, I realized: We are all storytellers. Continuously, we translate the experiences of our past and present into stories. Stories about ourselves, about the world, about others, about love and pain, about belonging and exclusion. About who we are and want to be, who stands in our way and who opens doors for us, why we do what we do and are who we are. These stories are neither false nor true, but many of them we repeat so often over time that they appear like the truth.

We do not always make ourselves the heroes or heroines in our own stories—some degrade themselves in their own life story to a secondary character, others to a victim, some embellish their stories, others are masters of omission and skipping. I still remember a moment at university when we students listened to a lecture by a well-known professor of our department. As is customary in academic procedure, he was introduced with the mention of all his glorious achievements, publications, and biographical milestones, and the longer his announcement lasted, the more impressed, but also intimidated, I, a first-semester student, sank into my chair.

When it was time for his lecture, the professor rose, stepped to the podium, and gave the room an honest smile. He thanked the presenter for her introduction, following the unwritten protocol of the academic habitus, and then said in essence: "When I hear announcements like this about me, I am sometimes quite impressed. And then I ask myself: Who are they actually talking about? You know, you have to be careful not to start retrospectively drawing a coherent picture from your CV, a straight path—as if there had never been any confusion, as if everything had always just worked out for you, as if you had never doubted yourself, as if you had always known exactly what you were doing. Don't be fooled. It's only the highlights that go into a CV, not the desperate moments between the entries."

N. Plohr, *Mindful Leadership*, https://doi.org/10.1007/978-3-658-48300-5_4

To be honest, I can't remember the lecture he gave afterwards, but these catchy and honest words, which I quote here from memory (and thus tell a story myself), have accompanied me ever since.

Beyond lecture halls and academic customs, we all continuously tell the story (or stories) of our lives. These narratives also include the inner critics I wrote about in the last chapter. But they are only part of the spectrum of voices and moods we carry within us. These continuous streams of thought that line up in our heads and bundle into stories. These stories often have a strong effect on our self-perception and the perception of others—even, or especially when we are not aware of them. Brené Brown goes so far as to write: "When we deny our stories, they define us."[1] Similar to the inner critics, the stories we carry within us and tell ourselves do not simply disappear just because we do not explore them. On the contrary—the more we try to turn away from them, the more they determine our actions, the more they define us.

In the context of coaching practice, I first came into contact with the power of our self-narratives during a training to become a sports mental trainer. The so-called self-talk regulation is a mental technique used by performance athletes to not only perceive the inner voices but also to regulate them in an empowering way. If you observe athletes in decisive moments for them, for example at the Olympic Games, you will be able to see this technique in action. There, conjuring words are spoken towards the pole before the pole vault, quiet conversations are held with the discus, or loud self-motivation is combined with tapping the body before stepping into the starting blocks.

You don't have to chase Olympic medals to apply this technique to yourself. Because let's be honest: These inner voices are sometimes quite loud. And they don't always see the world as it is. And they are not always encouraging, confident motivators.

Rather, they try to embed everything we experience in a familiar and meaningful context and often resort to narratives that find their origin in past experiences. We carry these stories into our relationships, into private and professional environments, into recurring and new situations we are confronted with. Regulating our inner storytellers, but also first and foremost consciously perceiving the stories they have in store, can not only help and empower us in sports, but also in corporate and private environments.

Many of the stories we tell ourselves about ourselves begin with: "I am good at..." or "I can't do xyz..." Others formulate a more general "That's just the way I am." Or even a: "That may be something for others, but not for me." These stories can range from preferences for certain foods or activities to personality structures and roles that we do not allow ourselves because the story we tell ourselves about ourselves does not permit it. Often, people in our environment are involved in our stories and we invent certain roles for them, imagining, for example, what they

[1] Brown, Brené: Rising Strong, London 2015, p. 267.

would probably say if we said this or that and then we would say that in response and then they…etc.

Presumably, we have all once been caught in the drama of this inner script, in which not only very concrete sentences for imagined conversations are designed, but also certain behaviors of our environment are translated into stories about people that never come true. In the attempt to appropriate the world and sort it out for ourselves, many narrative threads quickly get mixed up. This is very human, but at the same time also an invitation to untangle these stories, to question them for their truthfulness and perhaps (and here I follow Brené Brown again)—to write a different ending to them.

An example of this process is the story of a client with whom I have been working for several years now. She came to me because she wanted to lose weight and bring more movement into her life. I started doing personal training with her once a week. Over twelve months, she lost fifteen kilos—even more impressive than her physical development, is the way she talks about herself and others. The woman I met almost two years ago often said: "I don't know if I can do this." She always seemed to be on guard against being excluded or disliked because of her body weight. We started gently, did many repetitions of the same exercises and movements, and she gained more and more confidence in her new body feeling. The sentence "I don't know if I can do this" was increasingly replaced by an "Ok, I'll try it."

A big topic from the beginning was her desire, but also her doubts, to be able to go jogging. I promised her that we would gradually increase the training and I was sure that she could go jogging with continuous progress. Exactly one week ago today, we completed the fifth running session together and I can hardly put into words how happy it makes both of us to see that she can not only jog short distances in one go, but also do tempo changes and short sprints—and that without joint pain, cardiovascular problems or other complaints. After our first run together, a few tears flowed and she quietly told me: "…and my doctor always told me I would never be able to jog."

The story of the woman who would never jog has changed. She herself has rewritten the end of this story and has many times detached herself from the inner "I don't know if I can do this."

Another example of a typical self-narrative begins with the words: "If only first…" I have a friend who clung to this narrative for years. "Once I've bought a flat, then I'll be relaxed and happy." "Once I am running my own business, then I'll be relaxed and happy." "Once I've started a family, then…" Probably we all have such a friend or know similar tendencies from ourselves.

I call these stories reward deferral stories. They manipulate our happiness, because while moment by moment passes and we live our lives, our attention is focused on the goal not yet achieved. We spin a story of conditional happiness, which, as soon as the promising goal is fulfilled, shifts again. The story of the *if only first* is often so strong that it lets all happy steps and stages pass by without recognizing them as such.

As a final example, I would like to tell a personal story from my time as a doctoral student. I had already done several years of research and had been working hard, but had not yet started writing. The longer I put off writing the first sentence, the more impossible the whole undertaking seemed to me. After many colloquia and tough discussions about my topic, my writing style, my approach and many frustrating experiences with criticism from all corners of my academic entanglements, the narrative had established itself in my head: "I can't do this. I'm just not smart enough. I will never finish my dissertation." I hadn't written a single word yet and yet I felt like I had already failed internally.

Because the pressure and fear of failure were so great, I pushed the whole topic away from me for several weeks. I had just moved to Hamburg and was going through huge changes in many areas of my life. I knew my doctoral position would soon expire and if I hadn't made it by the end of this employment, I would never make it.

Time was also running out for me in a very concrete way. The only thing that calmed me down and distracted me during this time was stand-up paddling. And it was—to my great fortune—one of the best summers we've had in Germany in recent years. I paddled up and down the Alster, explored the Hamburg canals, familiarized myself with the city, always on the move and in motion. Sometimes I was on the board early in the morning and felt so free and light that I could hardly believe it myself. And then there was this one morning when I pushed off from the dock, started paddling, and suddenly knew how I could approach my topic in a new way. In a way that would make me enjoy writing the work. I remembered again what fascinated me about my topic, about writing, about thinking and researching. Behind all the narratives of the past years, behind all the "I can't do it anymore, I can't manage, I'm not good enough", there was another voice. And it spoke of the joy of thinking, of writing, and also of all the moments of success that I had already experienced. My inner "I can't do this" and "It's too difficult" became an "I will try. And it may bring me joy."

The three examples mentioned are self-narratives. Stories that we knit about ourselves and that, often also influenced by our environment, become ingrained in us. If we do not actively turn to these narratives and allow ourselves to reshape them or write them a different ending, they may even become our life stories. Or as Brené Brown puts it: *"When we deny our stories, they define us"*.[2]

Practice: Storytellers

Listen to your inner voices as if they were storytellers. Whenever you can, pay attention to which stories repeat themselves in your head throughout the day—stories about you and others, your environment, situations and behaviors. Write them down. Maybe for some a keyword is enough. "The jogger". Or "not enough". Or "if only first".

---

[2] Brown, Brené: Rising Strong, London 2015, p. 267.

Read your stories and ask yourself: Are these stories really true? Can I rewrite them or give them a new ending? Do they limit me or give me strength? Are they stories from the past and is it perhaps time to let go of them?

If you find it difficult to let go of self-narratives, a mental technique called "thought stop" can help to start with. Whenever you notice that you are getting entangled in a story from which you want to free yourself, actively set yourself a stop sign. You can also say out loud: Stop! This interrupts the flow and embellishment of the narrative and reminds you that it is "just an (old) story." The active stopping creates a pause, a gap, which you can fill over time with new narratives. Narratives that correspond more to yourself and your phase of life. Narratives that you like to listen to.

Empathy

In psychology, empathy is defined as the ability to relate to, and resonate with the experiences of others.[1]

According to Davies, three types of empathy can be distinguished: Cognitive Empathy types, who can put themselves in the shoes of others in the form of a perspective change, but remain emotionally untouched. The Affective Empathy types, who mirror emotions as soon as they establish an empathetic relationship with others, regardless of what they themselves are currently feeling and experiencing. And the Social Empathy types, who can cognitively and emotionally put themselves in the shoes of others, but do not let themselves be overwhelmed by the feelings of others.[2]

Like any schematic division, this one also reduces complexity. Nevertheless, I introduce it here and invite you to do a self-check and ask yourself which form of empathy you are most inclined to. From my perspective as a sociologist and also as a coach, many other factors come into play that determine the relationship- and situation-specific form of empathy. Cultural factors, gender-specific role models and imitation processes, upbringing and experiences with a more or less empathetic environment, situation-specific variables and also empathic capacity as a matter of one's own energy resources—all this can be included in the differentiated analysis of empathy.

For competencies in the area of Inner Leadership and Mindful Leadership, empathy is a key to many doors at once. It is no coincidence that empathy workshops are piling up in business coaching contexts, as well as in the area of personal development.

---

[1] Stangl, W. (2021). Keyword: *'Empathy—Online Lexicon for Psychology and Pedagogy'*. Online Lexicon for Psychology and Pedagogy.: https://lexikon.stangl.eu/1095/empathy (2021–12–02).

[2] Davis, Mark H. (1980). A multidimensional approach to individual differences in empathy. JSAS Catalog of Selected Documents in Psychology, vol. 10, pp. 85 ff. Davis, Mark H. (1983). Empathic concern and the muscular dystrophy telethon. Empathy as a multidimensional construct. Personality and Social Psychology Bulletin, vol. 9, no. 2, pp. 223–229. (Stangl 2021).

N. Plohr, *Mindful Leadership*, https://doi.org/10.1007/978-3-658-48300-5_5

In this chapter, I would like to consider some of the aspects and conditions of empathy mentioned above and apply them to the reflection of Inner Leadership. This chapter will also end with reflection questions that can be applied and discussed not only alone, but also in a team. As with the previous chapters and the entire structure of this book, I follow step by step the development from inside to outside.

What is implied in all three definitions of the empathy types according to Davies is a specific relationship to the ability to set boundaries. The Cognitive Empathy types, for example, keep their emotionality to themselves and penetrate the behavior and experiences of others more through a mental immersion in their counterpart. In this form of empathy, there are boundaries to communication about certain situations and especially feelings, because some moods, decisions or attitudes go far beyond the cognitive penetration of facts and touch inner states that are difficult to understand for very cognitively inclined people. Cognitive Empathy types make themselves less vulnerable in their style of communication and empathetic connection. This can lead to people being less open to them and holding back with emotional topics and levels, because they know that a purely cognitive viewing and exchanging is not enough for them. Their emotional range is simply not resonated with and can therefore only be difficult to become the subject of exchange.[3]

The Affective Empathy types, on the other hand, set very little to no emotional boundaries, which can go so far that they no longer feel themselves and their situation because they let themselves be overwhelmed by the emotionality of others. Here, another boundary is drawn or disregarded. The emotions of others, from which the Cognitive Empathy type excessively distances himself, in this case wash over one's own emotions and emotional states. In place of the underrepresented emotional empathy for others, here comes the excessive emotional empathy for the same.

I had a friend to whom the latter applied very strongly. It went so far that I sometimes had to comfort and build her up again after I had shared something with her for which I actually needed comfort and support myself. She mirrored my fears and worries in such an intense way that over time I withheld from her that level of my emotional state in order to protect her and me from the consequences.

Empathizing and sympathizing takes a lot of energy—of course, something also comes back if it is a balanced exchange of mutual openness and healthy demarcation. However, if the other person reacts to one's own suffering with even more suffering, it becomes increasingly difficult to maintain the energy balance or even to emerge strengthened from conversations.

Excessive empathy for others is, contrary to many conventional assumptions, not always free of self-centeredness, as this example shows. If the goal of empathy

[3] This observation touches many levels that will be deepened in the second part of the book, for example under the topic of metacommunication and especially vulnerability as a basic building block of Mindful Leadership.

is to hold space for the other person and enable openness to go into exchange about the other person's emotional state, it helps no one to fill this space with one's own mirrored emotions and thus rob the actually needy person of space and energy.

It can be positively noted that types of affective empathy are also sensitive to the beautiful aspects of the emotional spectrum. However, for the exchange and reach of empathy, this could mean that negative moods are consciously withheld, thus limiting open conversation once again.

Balanced and progressive is the definition of the third type. Both cognitively and emotionally empathetic, and at the same time capable of distinguishing between one's own inner states and those of the other person. Balance is always an act, a process, and constant adjustment—balance never stands still, but is only describable as balance because it is not static and never final. This also applies to the continuous balancing of cognition and emotion, self- and other-empathy, as well as the expansion and boundary drawing regarding empathic capacity.

Following the traces of this balance, I would first like to turn my gaze inward and not only differentiate the ability to empathize in relation to others, but also in relation to oneself. My observations in coaching sessions with clients, but also in conversations with work colleagues and friends, show that it is not always easy to feel into oneself and develop empathy for one's own confusions and entanglements. Many women with whom I enter into conversation in coaching tend to have more empathy for others (other-empathy) than for themselves (self-empathy). This is an observation that does not want to fall back into a gender dualism, but at the same time takes into account the narratives and experiences of many women in my environment.

Women's rights activist Gloria Steinem refers to this tendency as *empathy-sickness*[4] and attributes the over-caring for others while neglecting one's own needs primarily to cultural conditioning. Girls are taught from a very early age how to care for others and that it is the desired behavior to be considerate or to act in the interest of a community and not primarily to assert one's own interests. One might consider these observations outdated in a culture of gender-neutral language and diversity—but the narratives of my clients and friends do not suggest that this tendency towards over-caring, excessive empathy, and feelings of shame regarding one's own needs has significantly changed.

I myself had a tearful aha moment in a coaching session that I was able to take advantage of during my doctoral studies and that was a turning point for me in many ways. My coach, a woman, gave me the space to talk about a colloquium in which I had to deal not only with criticism of my presentation, but also with upcoming, humorously intended remarks from the male professors. From an outside perspective, the situation was "no big deal", but inside me, shame and guilt and the feeling of being a helpless twelve-year-old again remained. Instead of having compassion for myself, taking care of myself, and setting boundaries, I fell

[4] Steinem, Gloria: Revolution from Within, Boston/Toronto/London 1992, p. 4.

into a self-reproaching conversation, full of doubts and accusations: "I should have prepared better. It was my fault. I just can't do it. I'm not smart enough for this." When we started to approach this situation in the coaching and to look more closely at the sentences that had been triggered in me, the self-doubt and sadness gradually turned into anger at "the others". My inner self-talk then sounded something like this: "Why do they do such a thing, they should know better, I will never talk to them again, what stupid, ..."

The inability in the specific situation to have compassion for myself and to set clear boundaries tipped over into an overreaction of demarcation afterwards. I had realized that I was not to blame, so now I was looking for a culprit out there. And thus switched from inner shame and guilt directly into defense mode. This gave me back my energy for a brief moment and also a fleeting sense of self-righteousness, but after a few minutes and with a look into the slightly smiling face of my coach, it suddenly didn't feel quite as good as in the moment of the outbreak.

She looked at me inquisitively and then calmly explained to me that empathy has two directions: one inward and one outward. I felt caught and seen at the same time. And she was so right. Empathy goes inward, to us, our inner life, and at the same time outward, towards others. If we manage to maintain this balance in both directions, we neither need destructive self-talk inside us, nor loud defense strategies outside. The balance between self- and other-empathy allows us to set clear and calm boundaries without inflating others into enemy images or degrading ourselves.

The differentiation of empathy types, which I listed at the beginning of this chapter, can also be further thought in terms of the balance of self- and other-empathy.

For example, if you tend to be very compassionate on an emotional level, sometimes even too much, it can be helpful to focus on your own cognitive analytical abilities and to analyze the situation based on facts and circumstances. As with the described exercise on the storytellers, a mental stop sign can help to pause and interrupt the pull into the over-emotional empathy, in order to then make a cognitive change of perspective.

Conversely, emotional empathy can be practiced by involving the body's sensing ability in the process of empathy. In practical terms: Bring your attention into your body while you listen to a story from your friend. Don't just listen with your head, but with every cell of your body. Also with your heart.

What fits here in a few lines is a continuous process of self-observation, which presupposes that one wants to deal more closely with the ability to emphasize. Although we are so close to ourselves in so many ways, it is often hardest for us to really empathize with ourselves and develop self-empathy. Without a certain sense for our own emotional life, we will only partially succeed in empathizing with others. I am always surprised that so many of my clients, regardless of gender, social status, education level, and age, are so little empathetic with themselves. Most of them lead a continuous negative self-talk, that lacks compassion. Many are shocked when they write down and read the inner critics, how harshly they judge themselves.

I am convinced that this tendency is connected with what Brené Brown describes as *culture of never enough*[5]. The constant perceived lack, according to Brown, can never be appeased by striving for "more", but demands a paradigm shift towards what she calls "wholeheartedness"[6].

I remember exactly how long I carried this feeling of "not being enough" with me (and in the spirit of sincerity: often enough still do) in the belief that I was the only person in the world who felt this way. Only when I started talking to friends about this belief long after my teenage years, we realized half laughing, half crying: We all had this sentence deeply stored in us and hid it from others out of shame, guilt, and competitive thinking. It felt for a long time as if openly sharing this sentence "I think I'm not enough" was an embarrassing admission and further evidence that it would probably be true. An admission of insecurity in a world that rewards and applauds loud, self-confident performers. It was such an incredible relief to share my own insecurity and even more to realize: Everyone knew it. I hear this sentence of not being enough in podcasts, in social media, in my professional and private environment, from people who from the outside seem to "have everything", from people in leadership positions who are seen by their employees as brimming with self-confidence, from beautiful women and stunningly attractive men, even from children and also from my students, who often feel too ignorant in their efforts to get good grades.

When I read about the *culture of never enough* in Brené Brown, I found this term apt and worrying at the same time. How did we become this culture? As a sociologist, I have learned that answers are often found in the many micrological moments and practices we go through every day. From evaluation schemes of the education system to physical norms and beauty ideals, from digital like economies in social networks to the self-tracking bracelet on the wrist, from family expectations to daily information overload and recognition mechanisms to the capitalist logic of "more is more"—How should we not think in this network of demands, overloads and striving for recognition that it is never enough? That we can never be enough?

We need, so my feeling, more spaces and more forms of expression for the open handling of the feeling of inadequacy. From my own experience I can say: Nothing has been as healing as the moment when I was allowed to learn that I am not alone with this feeling at all, on the contrary, that it is the exception to meet people to whom this feeling appears unknown.

The courage to make oneself vulnerable and open the conversation has been worth it every single time. The external and internal fronts become softer, where there was competition and tension, laughter and loosening are possible.

[5] Brown, Brené: Rising Strong, London 2015, p. 274.

[6] Ibid.

And once again, space for empathy. With oneself and the other. I am convinced: The *culture of never enough* is a training ground for compassion, for humor in dealing with mistakes and for new encounters with oneself and others.

I would like to conclude this chapter with concrete reflection questions. Since it can be difficult to reflect on one's own empathy ability and a blind spot can naturally creep in, it is particularly helpful with these questions to involve trusted people and ask them for honest feedback. Perhaps this will also provide an opportunity to discuss the *never enough culture* and practice the revolutionary "always enough".

Reflection questions: Self- and other-empathy

1. On a scale of 1–10, how empathetic are you with yourself?
2. On a scale of 1–10, how empathetic are you with others?
3. Are you more of an affective, cognitive, or social empathy type? (especially here, feel free to check in with a person you trust)
4. How well can you set boundaries with others and their emotional states?
5. What can you learn from your ability to empathize with yourself for your compassion with others?
6. What can you learn from your ability to empathize with others for your compassion with yourself?
7. What role does the *never enough culture* play for you?

Practice: Connected Listening

In addition to the reflection questions, the exercise of connected listening can help to balance self-empathy and empathy for others. You can try it out for yourself without letting your counterpart know, or test it as a mutual, open experiment with partners, colleagues, and friends. The instructions for this exercise are incredibly simple, but the implementation is not always easy. Stay connected with your body while you listen to your counterpart. Focus on what your counterpart is saying, and at the same time be present in your body—for example, with your breathing, your inner space, your feet standing on the ground, or even with your relaxed facial muscles. By directing your focus to yourself and your conversation partners, you maintain self-perception and perception of others. You engage in the conversation and listening, but do not lose contact with yourself, your body, your feelings. Your body perception helps you to be more sensitive and compassionate overall, which can create a deep connection with your counterpart.

Self-Tracking

Building upon the concept of *never enough culture*, this chapter revisits my doctoral research and explores its connection to what I term *Inner Leadership*.

For those who have not yet come into contact with the topic of self-tracking, here is a brief definition: Self-tracking encompasses digital self-measurement facilitated by devices such as wearables, smartphones, and specialized applications. Most often, users document their movement or sleep behavior. Metrics like heart rate, daily steps, and calorie expenditure are also commonly tracked. More and more women are using apps to track their cycle, and some of my clients also use so-called mood tracking, where the mood is recorded daily and users are asked to pause briefly and ask themselves: How do I feel today?

When I started my doctoral research on self-tracking in 2015, the tracking watch on the wrist was still more of a fringe phenomenon. When I published the book on my research at the beginning of 2021[1], not only the technology but also the research on it had developed rapidly. It has now become part of a new normality to have one's body data continuously available, to look at the watch, not only to check the time, but also to read all other self-affirmation data.[2]

Aha. Saturday, 9:30 am, 2300 steps, heart rate of 62, calorie consumption 300. Such short, number-based impulses and self-narrations occur repeatedly throughout the day in self-tracking and are incorporated into a larger self-image designed based on the collected data.

The problem is that the goals set at the beginning can be continuously shifted, and thus the feeling of not being enough can set in again and again. Self-tracking is a practice that brings the main impulse of a *never enough culture,* namely the

---

[1] Plohr, Nikola: What is Selftracking? An Autoethnography of the Measured Self, Bielefeld 2021.

[2] "Normality" is always culturally made, subject to continuous change and societal readjustments. Self-tracking is a practice that comes with privileges. Those who can afford the corresponding technology and also have the time to deal with themselves so intensively belong to a minority that can afford this "normality" as such at all.

N. Plohr, *Mindful Leadership*, https://doi.org/10.1007/978-3-658-48300-5_6

urge for constant improvement, so close to the body that over time, users can hardly escape the pull of this practice. In a multi-year self-experience, I was able to observe this, as it was reflected back to me in interviews and research. Many shared that, over time, they focused solely on step counts and calorie numbers, allowing self-tracking to dominate their thoughts and routines, leading to a persistent feeling of inadequacy.

Reflecting on my self-experiment and extensive engagement with the topic, I identify compelling opportunities for cultivating *Inner Leadership* through self-tracking. I am convinced that one reason for the great fascination with self-tracking is the opportunity to be given a clear task, to be able to be led in a certain way, but also to feel a sense of self-efficacy when achieving set goals.

One question that has repeatedly occupied me in the analysis of self-tracking was that of *agency,* the power to act. Because while self-tracking is about exercising control over one's own body and self-design, this control, this power to act, is constantly handed over to the device, to the technology. Over time, my observation is that the initial pleasure in self-documentation tips into the feeling of being controlled. Self-tracking is also the perfect projection surface for all self-narrations and inner critics that existed before the practice began. This requires a reflective stance towards self-tracking, a kind of meta-observation of the practice.

When clients enthusiastically tell me they have discovered self-tracking for themselves, I always recommend first setting a clear goal for which the use of self-tracking makes sense, secondly defining a fixed period in which the practice is applied, and thirdly repeatedly observing one's own attitude towards self-tracking and honestly asking oneself: Is this really (still) good for me?

This final point functions as a kind of meta-tracking, aligning with my Interpretation of Inner Leadership: The capacity to guide make decisions, and establish direction. I am convinced that a major factor in the fascination around the topic of self-tracking is that one leaves the direction to the technology and feels like one can finally lean back internally because the app already tells one what to do. I observe that this is another form of externalization of responsibility, which, if one is not completely clear about it, is directly washed back and shows itself as an exercise of control.

When asked whether self-tracking is beneficial or detrimental, my response is invariably: It depends. On the one hand, on the points I have already mentioned, on the other hand, on how strongly the users have cultivated a form of Inner Leadership that allows them to clearly reflect and classify their own practice. If neither a clear goal is formulated, nor regularly reflected, nor Inner Leadership is practiced, the danger is very great to get caught in the pull of self-tracking and to live according to the rhythm of the tracking watch.

The reason I am integrating this topic here is another. Besides the negative effects that self-tracking can have, I find it fascinating how strong the interest in documenting one's own body, health, and everyday habits is and I wonder on a somewhat broader level: What else can self-tracking be? How can self-tracking be thought of differently and translated into the confrontation with inner leadership strength?

Self-tracking in technology-based offerings mainly refers to the body. Calories, steps, heart rate, etc. What I notice again and again in my work as a personal trainer and coach: When clients come to me with a "body goal" such as "losing weight" or "getting fit" or "running a marathon", there is usually another, sometimes unconscious, sometimes quite obvious issue behind the body goal. Being loved. Being beautiful. Proving perseverance. Behind these issues often lie further layers and stories that can be projected onto the body level, but go far beyond it.

Body goals are not bad per se, sometimes even necessary, and self-tracking can be used very well to achieve these goals—but I usually see long-term changes in clients who also become aware of the other issues linked to their body (image). And who also keep an eye on their self-tracking behavior and repeatedly make room for reflection on the practice.

When I analyze the fascination for self-tracking and summarize it in a few points, the following incentives can be observed:

1. The feeling of self-efficacy, which sometimes already begins with downloading an app and getting a colorful graphic with your own data. This follows a bit the logic of the New Year's registration boom in fitness studios.
2. The feeling of self-control while at the same time leaning back internally and handing over responsibility to the technology that sets the pace. This is where a paradox is rooted, as it runs through practice on many levels. External and self-control intertwine.
3. A satisfying form of discipline, at least in the initial stage, which can turn into over-disciplining and strictness, but can also be maintained as healthy self-discipline.
4. The visible documentation of progress, which is not only available to oneself but can also be presented to others.
5. The intense focus on a topic or a specific goal, which is not to be underestimated in times of diverse distractions. This can be relaxing because the energy is bundled and does not meander so easily, but it can also lead to tunnel vision and a neurotic-looking focus on numbers, data, and statistics.

This last point in particular has repeatedly struck me in my research, interviews, and also in self-observation. With the focus on self-tracking practice, the daily, sometimes even hourly reminders of the goal to be achieved, the self-image increasingly narrows down to the one topic or goal. Many told me that over time they could think of nothing else but self-tracking, their steps to be taken, constantly their gaze wandered towards the tracking bracelet. In these moments, the focus on tracking constantly interrupts all other activities and subordinates them to the self-tracking goal. This is largely due to the technology, which, always within reach, reminds itself with vibration signals and push notifications. The frequent glance at the smartphone is then additionally supplemented by an at least equally frequent glance at the smartwatch. The self-control, the focus, the self-efficacy can tip into feelings of restlessness, inner unrest, and dissatisfaction due to the constant interruption.

Another point of criticism on my part is the constant generalization of goals, (beauty and fitness) ideals, which are inscribed into the tracking apps and watches. Every body is different. Health is so much more than just the compilation of a few key figures. We are constantly changing, for example, depending on the form of the day and also hormonal fluctuations depending on gender. Most tracking offers do not sufficiently take into account this individuality, but are primarily aimed at continuously coupling users to the technology and generating data sets.

To account for the fascinating aspects of self-tracking and at the same time consider the critical observations mentioned, I would like to present a few ideas on how self-tracking can also be used for the cultivation of Inner Leadership. I myself use the technique of journaling to focus inward every day and record how I am doing, what concerns me, what ideas and visions I have. Sometimes I also collect quotes from books that particularly inspire me. By now, whole books of these notes are piling up, which I occasionally read to inspire myself or to look for (old) patterns. I do not use a fixed form for this, but simply write "just like that". The previously mentioned Free Writing can also be a form of self-tracking, a written self-documentation of inner thought streams. If you carry out this practice for a certain period of time and then delve into the self-collected "data" again, new insights often emerge.

In a podcast, I picked up the idea of noting down "the best of the day" or "the most remarkable of the day" every day.[3] Writing is a simple and at the same time powerful technique that can be used in line with the individual goal. For example, a client of mine writes down three keywords every morning to document his emotional state. This small moment of "check-in", of self-observation, has now become an integral part of his self-care and counteracts his tendency to forget his needs due to work. With this technique alone, he is better able to maintain his boundaries, take breaks, and intervene earlier when he is at risk of overloading himself.

A family with whom I conducted personal training sessions put a marble in a large vase for each training session and, as soon as it was full, went to the sea together. A client who was practicing a gentler view of herself stuck a small heart on her mirror every morning when she found herself beautiful. The glue was very difficult to remove later, but—the principle still worked.

What the examples mentioned share is the clear visualization of what is actually invisible. Small changes like the regular conscious and loving look in the mirror are given a visible framework through individual self-tracking and are linked to a self-chosen reward principle. This is, just like the independently formulated goal, much more individually tailored to one's own needs than the pre-programmed structures of an app can do.

In addition to feedback conversations with valued people, self-tracking is a very helpful tool for getting to know oneself better, pursuing concrete goals,

[3] Thanks to Hotel Matze, the podcast by "Mit Vergnügen" with Matze Hielscher.

and documenting changes. Everyone who wants to expand their inner leadership strength, decision-making and reflection skills is warmly invited to just give it a try.

The self-tracking approach proposed here requires no app—just time, chosen materials, and a bit of creativity. Before we get into the self-made self-tracking practice, here are a few preparatory tips:

1. Formulate a clear goal and take a short (or slightly longer) time to think about the "goal behind the goal". Write them both down and keep them so that you can read them again at the end of your tracking phase.
2. Determine a clear period for self-tracking. I would choose at least four weeks and at most three months for the beginning.
3. Find a rhythm for your self-tracking practice—determine a time of day that allows you to "track" with little effort. For example, I always write in my diary in the morning, but the evening is also excellent for recording a specific daily goal or reviewing the day.
4. Make it as easy and joyful as possible for yourself to practice self-tracking.
5. Reflect regularly on whether and how you want to continue tracking.

Exercise: Selfmade-Selftracking

Once you have clearly defined and formulated your goal, consider what type of visualization suits you and your topic. Maybe you prefer numbers to language—then it makes sense to set up a small table and work with scales, for example. An example: On a scale of 1–5, how comfortable did I feel in my body today?

Use a form that is easily accessible to you. If you practice with the "glass principle", choose one that you like and place it in sight. Maybe you don't want marbles, but chestnuts, stones, small notes, or something completely different. Maybe you don't like the "crafting" at all, but prefer a form of targeted journaling or even an Excel spreadsheet. Create a structure for yourself that makes it easy for you and takes little time. Maybe a sentence a day (what was good today?) or three keywords about the day's feelings. Or a number.

Self-tracking can be so much more than what apps suggest to us. Self-knowledge. Self-reflection. Personal development. Change. Find your form, one that is good for you and corresponds to your nature. And if you feel inspired now: Just give it a try.

Self-Efficacy

Whether in sociology or psychology, in coaching contexts or lecture halls, the term and concept of self-efficacy frequently emerge in my encounters. Whether due to my personal interest or its relevance as a contemporary trend—it was evident from the inception of this book that self-efficacy would play a central role.

Self-efficacy refers to the belief in one's ability to influence external events through personal actions. Instances such as the successful execution of plans, the realization of intrinsic interests, the environment's response to one's action, and the materialization of ideas—all encapsulate the essence of self-efficacy. In 1977, psychologist Albert Bandura established the foundational concept of self-efficacy expectation, laying the groundwork for subsequent research and application. According to Bandura, the experience of being able to achieve a certain effect influences a basic attitude of self-efficacy expectation. In short: the more experiences of efficacy I collect, the higher is my expectation to be able to repeat this efficacy in different situations: "Efficacy expectations therefore influence how people think, how they feel, how they motivate themselves and how they act."[1]

A simple example: If I enter job interview with an inner belief of "I can't do it anyway", it will be difficult for the interviewer to see a creative, self-confident employee in me. However, if I have a high expectation of self-efficacy, which is based on certain experiences from the past, I go into the situation with an inner attitude of "I can do this and I am looking forward to the challenge". The reaction to a possible rejection also varies depending on the expectation of self-efficacy. If the inner attitude is already oriented towards failure from the outset, the experience of rejection will be added as a confirmation and the inner "I knew it wouldn't work" will be reinforced. With a high expectation of self-efficacy, the reaction to the same rejection can go in a completely different direction. For example, to a

[1] Albert Bandura, quoted from Rosa, Hartmut: Resonance. A Sociology of World Relationship, Berlin 2016, p. 271.

N. Plohr, *Mindful Leadership*, https://doi.org/10.1007/978-3-658-48300-5_7

"Ok, it wasn't meant to be. I'll try somewhere else and in the end I'm sure I'll find a job that suits me even better."

In coaching contexts, these tendencies of mindset and the anticipations of certain behaviors are also referred to as *self-fulfilling prophecy*. The prophetic intuition feeds less from a divine inspiration or fate than from the fact that all actions and ways of thinking, including body language and charisma, react to this inner conviction. If the holistic appearance, formulation and action is oriented towards efficacy, it follows a different inner conviction and power than if no trust is given to one's own efficacy.

For some critics, this may now sound as if one had to be brimming with expectations of self-efficacy all day long and then everything would succeed. This often reflects on over-simplifications in coaching contexts, when morning affirmations are to be spoken in front of the mirror (I am great!), in order to enforce an expectation of self-efficacy. The crux is that these sentences can be recited as diligently as they want—if the subconscious has stored other experiences, there will always be a dissonance between feeling and reciting, which tends to undermine the trust in the view of the self even more.

This also touches on a somewhat broader misunderstanding regarding the expectation of self-efficacy, which Hartmut Rosa illuminates in his book "Resonance. A Sociology of World Relationship". As a sociologist, Rosa is less interested in the affirmations in front of the mirror than in the consequences of the expectations of self-efficacy on the relationships we enter into with the (surrounding) world and other people. In his book *Sociology of World Relationships*, he focuses on the relationship between self-efficacy and resonance experience.[2]

According to Rosa, there is a serious misunderstanding in that the culture in which we live equates self-efficacy with possession and, as a result, acts more result-oriented than process-oriented.

Self-efficacy does not mean owning more objects, having a lot of money, or conforming to an external concept of success. Rather, self-efficacy is the feeling of being able to make a difference in this world, to be able to create something, and to be in a resonant, vibrating, energy-charged relationship with this world. This attitude can naturally lead to material possessions and success, but it will tend not to define itself through materialism, but rather find expression through the process of acting and creating. Instead of following an external concept of success and the accumulation of possessions, self-efficacy serves intrinsic motivations that arise from the body, the mind, the joy of creating. This feeling has been proven to affect our entire body and is one of the most effective means of preventing stress and anxiety symptoms, which in turn are considered the main triggers of most diseases in industrialized nations.[3] Burnout and depression, to name just two of the exhaustion diseases of our time, often arise from the feeling that one's own actions and

---

[2] Cf.: Rosa, Hartmut: Resonance. A Sociology of World Relationship, Berlin 2016, p. 269 ff.

[3] Rosa, Hartmut: Resonance. A Sociology of World Relationship, Berlin 2016, p. 281.

creations have no effect and do not reach the world. Hartmut Rosa calls this "mute world relationships"[4], in which the environment seemingly no longer responds to anything that is sent.

In quantum physics, this sphere of influence that people experience around them is referred to as the quantum field. Nowadays, research is being conducted at universities around the globe on the energetic frequencies that surround a body, a consciousness.[5] Every single cell of our body has a certain frequency, which constantly aligns, adapts, and reorients itself with the environment. Depending on how strong the inner alignment is, the energetic field of the body is influenced or not by external impulses.

Have you ever sat in a subway car on a Monday morning feeling good and full of energy? Felt the stress, the fatigue, perhaps also isolated positive excitement around you? Did you get off the train the same way you got on? With the same energy? Did you have to set boundaries, perhaps put on headphones, turn up the music, to maintain your own frequency?

Hartmut Rosa also uses many examples of resonance that have to do with music. Not without reason, it is easy for us to imagine frequencies and sound waves when it comes to music, and to imagine certain moods they can put us in. In principle, as it can be transferred to our world relationships, our environment is always playing music. But we don't always like the same genre.

In the mode of self-efficacy, the feeling arises of playing music as part of an orchestra and joyfully letting one's own notes flow into the overall work of art. This interplay can be wonderfully transferred to teams and groups. Because self-efficacy is even potentiated when others resonate with us on the same frequency.

According to Hartmut Rosa, individuals not only feel self-efficacious, but in the collective they even feel *world-efficacious*.[6] The feeling of being able to achieve anything, to reach anything, is intensified in groups that align themselves towards similar goals and influencet each other with their euphoria. Not without reason, mass psychology takes this phenomenon of contagion as the starting point for critical perspectives on collective experiences, which in German history did not always have positive effects. Euphoric masses united in the collective feeling of world-efficacy can take violent, oppressive, and radical paths. This gives rise to the justified fear that the critical individual could dissolve in the mass, throw all reason overboard, and only act guided by feelings. On the other hand, group experiences of efficacy, energy exchange, and power, which according to Hannah Arendt unfold moments of *being able to shape*, cannot occur alone. Arendt considers modern individualism to be alienated and *world-poor*.[7]

---

[4] Ibid. p. 315.

[5] Among others: Jain, Shaminin: Healing ourselves: Biofield science and the future of health, Colorado 2021.

[6] Rosa, Hartmut: Resonance. A Sociology of World Relationship, Berlin 2016, p. 275.

[7] Hannah Arendt, quoted from: Rosa, Hartmut: Resonance. A Sociology of World Relationship, Berlin 2016, p. 275.

As so often, individual and collective self-efficacy is also about balance and the right measure. On a somewhat more practical level, it can be observed that sharing and making self-efficacy visible can trigger both envy and resentment, as well as inspiration and motivation in others. In team coaching, I repeatedly notice how much the individual actors hold back with their successes to avoid negative reactions or to not appear arrogant. However, this avoidance behavior also leads to others not being given the chance to enjoy or be inspired by one's own self-efficacy. In the startup scene, on the other hand, it is widespread to celebrate and make even the smallest progress visible. This can sometimes seem exaggerated, but it regularly offers the opportunity to create visibility for individual and collective self-efficacy—and even if a toast is made to the maintenance of the office plants, the space is created to establish a culture of recognition together.

Rarely have I encountered employees in workshops who were completely satisfied with the feedback they received for their work. Because they usually received *no* feedback at all, no matter how well or mediocre they performed their tasks. It is an important part of self-efficacy to have one's own actions and creations confirmed—it is not primarily about being constantly applauded, but rather about getting any kind of response at all.

According to Hartmut Rosa, this search for a response is ultimately a search for a resonance experience, which here is closely related to an experience of self-efficacy. Both are interrelated, because if I am used to being self-efficacious, I will walk through the world more openly and confidently and correspondingly resonate with it. If, on the other hand, I feel little self-efficacy, not seen, alienated and powerless, no resonance can occur. I then simply lack the openness and also the courage to encounter the world and take my place in it.

For the development of Inner Leadership, self-efficacy is a key to many doors at once. A first step can be to become aware of one's own effectiveness and to take a closer look. So often in my coaching sessions, I encounter clients who do not find themselves effective, who feel they have not achieved enough or even that they are not enough. To counteract the *never enough culture* that continues within us, the view of one's own successes, one's own effectiveness is of enormous importance. Again, it is about a balanced balance: self-aggrandizement (often a learned protective armor out of fear of injury) is no more indicative of healthy self-confidence than the eternal belittling and ducking, which does not want to recognize its own greatness and is heavily dependent on the judgment of others. I often wonder why it seems so difficult to stand powerfully and authentically for one's own strengths and to share effectiveness in an inspiring way without elevating or belittling oneself and others.

I am convinced that collective and individual self-efficacy—and also making it visible—points a way out of the *never enough culture*. As so often, the cultivation of new, transforming approaches begins within ourselves. From the inside out, these new forces then pave their way. Into teams, into families and groups, and perhaps also into cultures.

To practically invite you to start with yourself, I would like to conclude this chapter with two small exercises. Again, this approach can also be transferred to teams—I will go into this in more depth in the chapter on metacommunication in Part II.

Exercise 1: The Self-Efficacy CV

Surely you have written a CV, a Curriculum Vitae, a resume before. Often educational degrees and professional stations find a place in it. Not always are these stations the greatest self-efficacy experiences we make in our lives. I still remember well how little proud I was in the end of my high school diploma. My grades were good, but somehow no fulfilling feeling set in, only relief to have mastered this section and to be able to turn my back on school. Quite different was the case with a play that I wrote, directed and performed together with my best friend in high school. To this day, it is one of my greatest self-efficacy memories, because it felt so right to pack all our issues into this piece, to rehearse secretly in the auditorium and to assert ourselves against all resistance. "Mrs. Plohr, you are about to graduate, you should focus on other things," said the principal and banned us from rehearsals, only to later adorn himself with the laurels of a successful premiere in front of the local press. A janitor stood by us during rehearsal time and let us onto the stage of the auditorium with shining eyes through the back door.

My journey through Australia after graduation was a strong self-efficacy experience—finding a job in Sydney, moving into a shared apartment, but also: leading happy relationships, maintaining friendships over long distances, learning to cook, standing the first wave while surfing, giving workshops, finally being able to keep houseplants alive, writing poems…

I hope you are like me and you are experiencing more and more moments of self-efficacy the longer you give yourself time to empathize, rather than ticking off a list of official, career-oriented stations, as most CVs contain. Remember moments when you were filled with the feeling of self-efficacy and you knew—this is right, there is an energy exchange, there is vitality and resonance. Perhaps you are experiencing self-efficacy in your life right now, perhaps in small, everyday moments, but perhaps also in huge projects.

Remember these big and small moments, write your self-efficacy resume. Were there times when it was just bubbling? When you often felt effective? What was good then? What was right? Who did you surround yourself with? Were others involved in these experiences?

When do you feel self-efficacious in your life right now? Who do you share these moments with?

Write your self-efficacy CV in your own way—it doesn't have to follow a linear course, it doesn't have to be chronological. It can follow your memory and your feeling. You can also use a mind map or mood board to familiarize yourself with your self-efficacy. You are doing this for yourself, because with this resume you don't have to apply or prove yourself anywhere. If you find it difficult to track down moments of self-efficacy, seek the advice of friends or family members. Often we are a little blind to our own effectiveness, but all the more trained in looking at that of others.

Exercise 2: Evening Routine Self-Efficacy Check
To cultivate your view of your self-efficacy daily, a kind of diary can be helpful, in which you note a short answer to the following question every evening: When did I feel self-efficacious today? At the beginning, you may still find it difficult to name such a moment of the day, but experience shows that this changes after a short time. As with so many topics, our view, our attitude towards them changes when we consciously deal with them and realign our focus. A routine or even a small ritual can be very helpful in this.

Rhythms, Rituals, and Routines

With that, I find myself already in the midst of the next chapter and topic of this book. Rhythms, rituals, and routines.

Christmas has just passed, the new year is still young, and the first discarded Christmas trees are piling up on the streets of Hamburg. This year, I had to smile as I tried to explain to my mother the tradition of the "Raunächte" and why I am using this time to prepare for the new year, including incense sticks, meditations, and wish lists for the coming twelve months. Her face revealed slight skepticism, perhaps even discomfort, but she held back and only said: "Oh, I don't know, these rituals are very foreign to me." Following my amused look, she too looked at the Christmas tree in the living room, the cookies on the kitchen shelf, the wreath adorned with candles on the dining table, the advent calendar on the stairs… And she couldn't help but smile. Rituals. A house full of rituals.

Especially during the Christmas season, they are so present, they are as important to many as they are not throughout the year. Associated with the dark season, the glimmer of candlelight, and family togetherness, Christmas gives many a rhythm, a sense of the passing and welcoming of a new year. Time to look back and forward, to take stock, to eat far too much and to move as little as possible. Let's be honest: For the majority of people in Germany, the religious significance of these days is increasingly fading into the background, while the ritual character remains unbroken.

Even if it rains at Christmas (not uncommon in Northern Germany), "Leise rieselt der Schnee" is sung fervently, more committed to tradition than to the eternally gray slushy weather. Nevertheless: Singing about the snow, decorating the Christmas tree and lighting the candles, baking and eating cookies—all this creates a ritual framework, a sense of recurrence and security in dynamic times of change.

Rituals are culturally embedded, often—but not always—tied to a specific period, repetitive practices to which people assign certain meanings, effects, and stories over a long period of time. Rituals provide a framework, they interrupt

N. Plohr, *Mindful Leadership*, https://doi.org/10.1007/978-3-658-48300-5_8

everyday life and give specific moments something special. They imply their own temporality and involve certain actions that are performed alone or together. Rituals often persist over many generations, create familial and cultural cohesion, enable inner reflection and moments of reflective pause.

Rituals are also closely related to the rhythms of nature and give us a sense of the course of a calendar year, a lunar cycle, or even a day. We all need these small breaks, practices that familiarize us with the inner and outer rhythms, so that the flowing time does not slip away, does not simply pass by. The smallest unit of recurring rhythmic practices that structure everyday life are our habits—also called *habits* in modern parlance.

As a sociologist, this definition reminds me of practice theory, in which practices are defined as the smallest unit of the social.[1] Like habits, practices are inherently repetitive. They have a specific form and contribute to the formation of social structures and systems through their recurrence. Practices encompass, similar to habits, the way we brush our teeth, cook pasta, or greet each other, as well as broader structures of work, living, and communication. What fascinates me about practices as well as habits is the power of these small, everyday actions that significantly shape our lives.

This chapter is an invitation to take a closer look at these micrological structures and to ask where and how change can begin. I want to try not to fall too much into the tone of the optimization imperative that swells up in my research on the topic. What are good and/or bad habits is in the eye of the beholder and in the network of relationships in which each individual is embedded. How strongly the evaluation of habits is subject to an ever-ongoing historical change is shown by a look at old talk show and interview formats, in which the protagonists smoke intellectually connoted in front of them and skillfully wrap mental clarity in gray cigarette smoke. In contrast, it borders on certainty that contemporary guides on the subject of habits define smoking as a habit to be overcome.

Habits are an essential part of what I call Inner Leadership and what can later also be applied to the team level and the topic of Mindful Leadership. In each case, targeted habits follow a process from inside to outside, from small to large. Every project, no matter how broadly conceived, every goal, no matter how high, is ultimately bound to the micrological implementation step by step. Often clients come to me with big goals and visions. "Be more successful", "Develop a fitter body shape" or "Become happier". No matter how large the idea of achieving a target state may be, ultimately the everyday practices and habits determine its implementation.

James Clear formulates the relationship between goals and habits as follows: "You do not rise to the level of your goals. You fall to the levels of your systems."[2] Even though such sentences sometimes make me uncomfortable, as it often

[1] Schatzki, Theodore: Social Practices—A Wittgensteinian Approach to Human Activity and the Social. Cambridge 1996, p. 89.

[2] Clear, James: Atomic Habits. London 2018, p. 28.

sounds like you just have to want something enough and bring enough discipline, then anything is possible (as a sociologist, this is too simplistic for me), there is a practical truth in it.

Just because I can dream and visualize big goals, they are not necessarily closer to me. The system, the bundle of practices and habits that I create and can fall back on, no matter how far the goal is (still) away, ultimately decides about the change process. This includes not only personal willpower and self-optimization strategies, but also the social environment, family imprinting, and the example set by the habits of others. James Clear points out that people are more willing to throw their good habits overboard than to isolate themselves from their own group. Shared habits bring with them a comforting feeling of belonging, which is why friendships and relationships of all kinds often rely on shared habits and mutually confirm each other in them. Anyone who wants to establish new habits is therefore always dependent on a system that supports the change at all levels—or at least does not prevent it. Anyone who has ever (New Year's or not) decided to abstain from alcohol, gluten or meat for a while and then gets invited to a summer barbecue knows exactly what I mean. "Oh come on, just one beer!" "Really, no meat? I couldn't do that! Isn't that boring, right?"

Most of the time, these persuasion skills fade over time, sometimes others are inspired and follow your own changes—but sometimes people remain stubborn and try with all their might to move you back to a "normal" behavior. It is precisely in these times of transition that it becomes apparent that normality is always made and only established in practices as such. When the new habits have shaped a new normality, then the critical phase is overcome.

There are very different views and statistics on how long it takes to establish new habits. James Clear comments on this in no uncertain terms and states that the introduction of new habits does not reach an end point. Even if I exercise regularly for twenty-five years, the habit only persists if I continue to do it. If I stop exercising, the practice is no longer system-relevant for me over time. Thus, the process of habit formation never ends—for all those who find this frustrating, it should still be noted that after a phase of establishment, new habits are easier to carry out. I have often been able to accompany this process in coaching and personal training. When clients no longer have to force themselves to train after a few weeks, but almost automatically put on their sports clothes and set off, a big step has been taken. The repeated execution of the same sequences simply leads to the brain drawing new paths and deepening them over time. It then feels more energy-saving to carry out the sports routine than not to do it, simply because the brain follows the familiar sequence and does not have to adjust to any new unexpected twists.

This point also reveals a danger of habit formation. The tipping point is often difficult to identify, but over time it can become increasingly difficult and almost impossible to simply do something different than the routine dictates. On this topic, I always have the popular fitness influencer Sophia Thiel in mind, who at some point would only order a spoon in the restaurant so she could eat her preplanned meal from a brought along Tupperware box. She now openly talks about the fact that this extreme adherence to routine not only harmed her physical, but also her mental health, on social media.

I sometimes wonder whether those very media platforms do not promote the over-controlling tendencies of the always same—the algorithm rewards regularity, the recreation of the always same, the commitment to certain aesthetics and rhythms. Likes confirm habits, confirm the familiar, the comfortably consumable, not the irritating, changing. This saves energy, at least that of the brain cells, but does not necessarily promote neuronal flexibility.

As is often the case, the topic of habits is about finding the right balance. Similar to the standing leg-playing leg logic, it is extremely helpful to integrate regular habits and routines into everyday life and at the same time maintain flexibility. This sounds super easy at first, but in practice it is a lifelong process.

To round off this chapter in a practical way, I would like to cite the four laws of habit formation according to James Clear and supplement them with a few reflection questions.

Practice: The Four Laws of Habit Formation (according to James Clear)[3]

1. **Make it obvious**
   A simple example: If you plan to go to the gym more often, it is helpful to lay out your workout clothes the night before the planned session and position them in such a way that you literally cannot pass them without at least having to glance at them.
   James Clear also reverses each law, so that the unlearning of "bad" habits is also incorporated into the process. Let's assume you not only want to exercise more, but also eat healthier, it can be enormously helpful to position sweets as inconspicuously as possible or to remove them completely from the household.
2. **Make it attractive**
   Especially at the beginning of establishing new habits, the chosen practice can seem very unattractive and it can be difficult to find motivation. Sticking with the sports example, one option would be to choose a particularly nice gym or to arrange a workout session with a friend. Since most nicer gyms also require a bit more membership fees, it is already "unattractive" not to go. Also, cancelling an appointment with a friend is "less attractive" than quietly throwing your own plans overboard.
3. **Make it easy**
   I often see clients who want to change everything from one day to the next and set goals that are hardly achievable for them or only with extreme effort. According to James Clear, it is extremely important to establish new habits in an easy and simple way. For example, starting with one push-up a day and not with a hundred burpees, to stay in the fitness paradigm.

[3] Clear, James: Atomic Habits. London 2018.

If you make it so easy to achieve a small goal and establish a small new habit, it is implicitly already very difficult to back out. Maybe there's not enough time and strength for a hundred burpees, but for one push-up?

Some people take the reversal of this law very far and make it very difficult for themselves not to carry out a habit. For example, people impose fines on themselves if they do not perform a workout, which is not only a striking example from James Clear's book, but even inspired a fitness app called Pact. With Pact, users set a certain amount of money that was deducted from their account if they did not train.[4] I don't know if one has to go that far, but I think the principle is particularly clear from these examples.

4. **Make it satisfying**

   Sometimes I feel that in the midst of the self-optimization craze, the joy of change is neglected. When establishing new sports habits, a favorite playlist can help—when introducing new eating habits, the enjoyable cooking and experimenting.

   Change doesn't have to mean self-denial or punishment. It can be fun to change oneself and everyday life and to pursue goals.

As already mentioned in the previous chapters, the practical examples can be applied not only individually, but also as a team. In particular, the first law—making changes obvious—and also the principle of small steps will play a role in the second part of this book.

To add another layer to these inspirations for establishing new habits, I would like to end this chapter with some reflection questions.

Reflection questions

1. Which of your habits do you like the most and strengthens you the most?
2. Which of your habits does not do this at all?
3. What has been preventing you from dropping or changing this habit so far?
4. What are internal and what are external obstacles in this?
5. How can you apply the four laws for the transformation of this habit?
6. On a scale of 1–10, how much are you living your rhythm?
7. What does the ideal daily rhythm look like for you?
8. What does the ideal annual rhythm look like for you?
9. What can you do/are you already doing to live it?
10. How easy/difficult is it for you to deviate from routines and habits?

---

[4] According to my research, the app is no longer available. Perhaps the logic of monetary self-punishment went too far for the users in the end.

People Pleasing

"Stop pleasing, start serving," my yoga teacher told me shortly after I completed my training in Traditional Hatha Yoga.

I will never forget how I stood in front of the group in my flowing, new yogi outfit, wanting to do everything right. The sun streamed into the beautiful yoga shala, built entirely in Balinese tradition from bamboo, a light wind blew and I felt completely in the right place at the right time. I led my class with a gentle voice, gave the group time to linger in the asanas and held back to give the participants space.

But my mantra-like chant couldn't mask my efforts. Yes, I wanted to please, wanted to do it right, do it well, pass and yes, get the confirmation from others that I was good enough to lead them. The comment from my teacher was clear and unequivocal: "You are a beautiful teacher, but have the courage not to please your students. Serve them, by leading them. Be present, be strong, be clear and you will hold much more space, much more energy in your classes. Stop pleasing, start serving."

His words resonated with me for a long time. What felt like a failure at first, over time developed into a full-fledged piece of advice for many of my tasks and roles. Whether as a lecturer, as a coach, as an author, as a yoga teacher, the sentence "stop pleasing, start serving" keeps echoing within me. Years later, I heard myself saying to a friend who works with teenagers, "Give them also the opportunity not to like you."

Of course, this does not mean to deliberately behave badly in order to train others in differentiation. Rather, the sentence reminds me that, first, it is impossible to always please and be liked by everyone—and second, that it is not my task to do so. It drains a lot of energy from the projects and activities and lectures and all situations in which I present myself in any way, if my attention is with the others and their (constructed by me) opinion about me. Instead of letting myself be distracted from myself and my activity, I practice again and again to stay with myself, with the actual task and not to make my self-feeling dependent on what others might think.

N. Plohr, *Mindful Leadership*, https://doi.org/10.1007/978-3-658-48300-5_9

What fits into a few lines here and is certainly familiar to many readers, is a (life-)long process that goes through new phases and brings shifting dependencies and liberations from old patterns. The fact that this topic is so (all-)present has several reasons. I would like to shed some light on two of them before I make the transition to the topic of Inner Leadership and leadership work in teams.

In psychology, human development and our behavior in groups are often traced back to the two basic needs of autonomy and security. On the one hand, we seek security in the protection of the social community, family affiliation and also in the formation of interest groups—on the other hand, we emancipate ourselves from these very things in order to perceive ourselves as autonomous and independent individuals. Dependence on others is not always negatively connoted, but means to enter into this protection, to give it as well and to enter into a safe relationship based on dependence. If we are susceptible to people pleasing, it often expresses the need for security, for protection and belonging.

On the other hand, we often want to free ourselves from these very security-promising ties, want to break the sometimes tight corset of belonging and go our own, new ways. This contains the second basic need of humans, the striving for autonomy, which carries the experience of being able to make independent and self-reliant decisions and to rebel against common opinions or at least to express criticism.

Both basic needs are equally important and essential for our lifelong development. The psychologist and author Stefanie Stahl writes in this context of an *autonomy-dependency conflict*[1], which is constantly fought out and always strives for an *inner balance*. It should be noted that this balance can only exist internally and cannot be established through an externally oriented number of followers or likes or other expressions of approval.

This brings me to the second point I want to highlight regarding people pleasing. Because in addition to the all too human autonomy-dependency conflict and the basic needs contained therein, which each generation deals with in its own way, our current time is additionally characterized by a constant public-visible carrying out of the same. Social media offer a platform, clear framework conditions and specific aesthetics to continuously present oneself as belonging, conforming and pleasing, but at the same time highly individual and unique.

The entire system of the like-economy of social media defines the thin line between autonomy and dependency, belonging and being different. The continuous translation of attention into likes, clicks, and comments invites one to engage in a spiral of people pleasing. What often starts with an individually designed profile, then follows more and more a logic of dependency on the self-created structures, which now want/need to be fed, served, and liked. When I talk to clients, students, lecturers, friends, I am confronted with the feeling of not being enough, which I

[1] Stahl, Stefanie: The child in you must find a home, Munich 2015, p. 38.

have already described under the keyword of the *never enough culture* and which tends to translate directly into people pleasing.

These tendencies become particularly when everyone in a relationship is trying to please the other and mutually seek security and belonging.

In psychology, this process is described as co-dependency. It occurs between lecturers and students, between mothers and daughters, fathers and sons, bosses and employees, and of course also in love relationships. In short, every relationship has the potential to become co-dependent when both sides try to please the other at all costs. The danger is that ultimately all involved actors lose the ability to act authentically and self-determinedly and instead match every behavior and every word with a constructed reaction of the other.

In such a relationship structure, authentic and self-connected communication is gradually lost, and a real exchange gives way to mutual pleasing. That this is neither attractive nor purposeful in the long run brings me back to the introductory quote. *Stop pleasing, start serving.* No relationship is served, no exchange nourished, when everyone involved gradually lose their own voice. In the permanent desire to please, both basic needs, security and autonomy, gradually dissolve. Because the more declarations of liking are generated, the more are needed to feel safe. And the more the perceived self-worth depends on declarations of liking, the less autonomy is dared.

The sociologist Hartmut Rosa, already quoted, repeatedly refers in his works to the constructive relationship between resonance and self-efficacy.[2] It is important for self-perception and external perception in relationships that both sides speak *with their own voice* and do not fade away in constructed echo chambers.[3] Encounter, resonance, is possible when difference is allowed and desired. This certainty, to be allowed to speak with one's own voice, opens the space for experiences of self-efficacy.

Even the heightened form of self-efficacy, the so-called flow, is very difficult to achieve when all attention is dedicated to people pleasing. Flow as the ultimate experience of self-efficacy is based on forgetting the outcome of the activity being performed and becoming so absorbed in the doing that it doesn't matter what others think of it or whether the result of the creation is liked. The process itself comes to the fore and the evaluation criteria of others move out of the conscious field of perception. Anyone who knows this feeling understands how invigorating it is to trust one's own creativity and to be guided from the inside out, rather than adapting to an externally constructed expectation. The constant external orientation and the desperate search for likes thus prevent the fulfilling feeling of flow, self-efficacy, and creative desire.

In this turning towards the inner joy of activities, an important aspect is contained for what I call Inner Leadership. Anyone who is always guided by the

---

[2] Rosa, Hartmut, Resonance. A Sociology of World Relationship, Berlin 2016.

[3] Cf.: Ibid. p. 282.

desire to please will easily overlook the inner voice, the inner joy of creative doing.

Of course, this does not mean that it doesn't matter at all what other people think about us and our behavior. As already justified with Stefanie Stahl, we need a constructive form of dependency on others, need exchange and feedback again and again, especially in the creative process. There is nothing reprehensible about striving for recognition from others and wanting to please to a certain degree. However, once again, I am concerned here with the already mentioned inner balance of dependency and autonomy, which is always forming and reshaping in a processual way.

So how does people pleasing relate to leadership positions? I would like to anticipate a little of the second part of this book, which draws on interviews to explore the topic of Mindful Leadership from various perspectives.

In preparation for the conversations that follow, I received an email with a wonderful rejection, which contained a reason for not being suitable as an interview partner and at the same time unintentionally provided material for this chapter.

I would like to mention that it is a woman who works in a chic apartment building and hotel in Hamburg and who, from an external perspective, undoubtedly holds a leadership position. However, she wrote to me the following: "[...] as a leader, I have too strong a need to be liked. That usually disqualifies me somehow."

I wonder if it necessarily has to be as C. P. writes? Isn't the desire to please one's team, one's employees, simply human to begin with? Don't the basic needs for autonomy and security also, perhaps especially, come into conflict in leadership roles? Not only for them personally, but also in relation to the team, the company, the brand, the product, or service? Doesn't entrepreneurship also live from the tension between freedom, creativity, innovation, and interdependence? I deliberately choose the term interdependence here, not dependence, to refer to the necessary space in between, the connection to other companies and actors in the market. The constructive form of dependence would be a form of co-creation, mutual reference, and productive difference that can occur within corporate structures, but also between competing providers.

Back to C. P. For me, her email is actually a prime example of what I understand by Mindful Leadership. Mainly because she reflects self-critically and openly on how her desire to please others affects her leadership qualities. This already takes a step that is often shied away from. This very step inward, towards conscious and chosen reflection, is essential to ensure not only for oneself but also in the team a space in which others can follow. The first step out of co-dependence is often taken by an actor in the relationship structure developing the ability to articulate this dependence and to lay it open for the others. As a result, other team members also have a point of reference to ask themselves: What is it like for me? Where do I hold back my needs, but also my creativity, and let myself be guided mainly by the desire to please?

It's OK to catch yourself people pleasing. It's important to become aware of specific situations and behaviors- and to continually seek balance.

And that's exactly why the unintended example from C. P. is one that speaks for Inner Leadership, for Mindful Leadership, and not for her self-described unsuitability to take on leadership.

Reflection questions on people pleasing and the autonomy-dependence conflict

1. How would you live if no one was watching?
2. How far does this way of life deviate from the one you are already pursuing?
3. Which need is more present in you right now, the need for security and belonging or the need for freedom and autonomy?
4. How "susceptible" are you to people pleasing?
5. In which areas of your life, in which relationship structures?
6. How does people pleasing manifest in you physically, mentally, psychologically?
7. Where do you observe people pleasing in your environment?
8. What can you do to give others the space to openly reflect on their people pleasing tendencies?
9. What do you need to bring your people pleasing into a healthy balance?
10. Is there a positive side to people pleasing for you?

Emotions

In exploring the link between emotions and leadership, I once again found Brené Browns insights to be valuable. She says, "I don't know any transformative highly respected leader who didn't study deeply his or her emotional patterns. Good leaders are highly self-aware."[1] Brené Brown sees it as a leadership skill, even indirectly as a condition for good leadership qualities, to learn to study one's own emotional patterns. It is noticeable here that she does not write about emotions, but about emotional patterns, that is, the specific chains of emotions and reactions on an emotional level that we all learn, develop and reinforce throughout our lives. For example, one person reacts to criticism with an angry defensive reaction, the next with fear and self-doubt, another with factual sobriety. To trace these patterns, to understand them and to dedicate an inner study to them, as Brown puts it, is essential not only for work as a leader, but in all variants of relationship structures.

The second part of the quote connects self-perception with the study of emotional patterns. This is interesting because it says something about the integrated perspective on the self. The self is thus significantly shaped and influenced by emotions and can only be researched as such when emotions and emotional patterns are taken into account.

In short: We are emotional beings and naturally also carry this essential part of ourselves into our professional activities. This awareness of emotion-related self-formation in work contexts was not always as relevant or visible as it is in our time. Richard David Precht notes that we live in a highly emotionalized society[2], in which even politicians and other professionals are not spared the question: And, how do you now feel with xyz?

---

[1] Podcast: Dare to Lead by Brené Brown: Episode Brené with Simon Sinek on Developing an Infinite Mindset, 18.01.2021, last accessed: 28.06.2022.

[2] TV format "Precht", Svenka Faßplöhler in conversation: Are we sensitizing ourselves to death, 04.12.2021, https://www.youtube.com/watch?v=OkaNritD8PM, last accessed: 04.03.2022.

N. Plohr, *Mindful Leadership*, https://doi.org/10.1007/978-3-658-48300-5_10

This emotionalization is a gain on many levels, but it also brings new challenges. Especially in New Work contexts, where flat hierarchies and a casual tone are cultivated, private and professional space, emotionality and objectivity require entirely new regulation and reflection mechanisms. Home office has further promoted these interconnections—when a job interview is conducted between a baby rocker and stacked dishes in the sink, or when a remnant of the argument at lunchtime still hangs in the air with the partner in the next room, it is only human to carry one's inner state even more into professional contexts. Of course, people have always brought these to work—but there were other regulations of what could be said and what could not be said, a stronger separation between public and private, and a habit of keeping to oneself when it came to emotional attunement at the workplace.

I think both forms have advantages and disadvantages and overall see the sensitization of society and the individual as a positive and progressive development. However, in this progress, the question arises as to what new skills and forms of reflection we need in order to be able to keep up with the change not only externally, but also internally.

Brené Brown, an expert in the field of emotion research, emphasizes in *Atlas of the heart* how important it is to be able to name emotions in order to better understand oneself and others.[3] While her book examines eighty-seven emotions and experiences in more detail, according to her studies, people are on average able to name only three: happy, sad, and angry.[4]

If we follow the assumption of sociology professor Eduardo Bericat, then the human experience of life is only possible with the involvement of emotions.[5] However, if we do not have a language for the emotions that enable us to access the world and its experiences, then the inner experience, understanding and classification of the world and our experiences remain extremely sparse and one-sided.

In my research for a relevant definition of emotion, I repeatedly encountered the statement that emotion researchers agree on only one point: that there is no uniform definition of emotions.[6] The fact that this lack of agreement in dealing with our emotional life is maintained up to the scientific level, in my view, is more of a gain than a loss. This way, our own inner inconsistency and subjectivity of feeling is taken into account more than with overly fixed, generally shared definitions.

I appreciate Brené Brown's approach, as she integrates experiences that lead to emotions into her atlas. As a result, not just three, but eighty-seven doors lead into one's own emotional life and also into the reflection of one's own patterns, consisting of situations, experiences, and emotions, which often intertwine in a seemingly impenetrable tangle.

---

[3] Brown, Brené: Atlas of the heart, New York 2021, p. xxiii.

[4] Ibid. p. xxi.

[5] Ibid. p. xxiii.

[6] Ibid. p. xxiv.

She highlights anger as a special, so-called secondary emotion. Thus, anger often hides a whole conglomerate of other feelings, such as fear, loneliness, shame, vulnerability, grief, overwhelm, and more.[7] Since I have been dealing more with the topic of anger, I can react better to it. Both when it is simmering within me, and when I am confronted with the anger of others. Instead of engaging in fiery arguments, it is easier for me to stay calm and meet my counterpart with empathy. What is really bothering this person right now? Why are they getting defensive? What part of them is trying to protect itself? If I am angry myself, I ask myself similar questions: What is behind my anger? Fear? Do I feel attacked, exposed, belittled?

Anger is important and can help us draw clear boundaries when others cross them. Anger is a strong emotion, energy in motion, that makes us stand up, perhaps even stand up for justice, and clearly express certain values.

I have a friend who advocates for gender equality and diversity—I got to know her as an often angry, incredibly eloquent student. Now she channels her anger into crystal clear articles, a PhD, and a years-long commitment as an equality officer.

Anger can be transformed into powerful creative potential. There is a story in my family that my grandfather sometimes deliberately provoked my grandmother, who painted a lot and very well, and once secretly told his children: "You have to make her really angry, then she paints the best pictures."

Whether this is the best instrument in the long run to stimulate creative work in the environment, I do not know. However, I am convinced that anger can ignite a fire and bring physical, creative energy into motion.

In the definition of emotions as *energy in motion*, there is a physical component of feelings that is important not only for dealing with anger, but also with all other emotional states. Emotions often bring very specific physical reactions with them. It is no coincidence that we speak of anger in the stomach, but also of butterflies in it, of the louse that runs over our liver or the lump of sadness in our throat, the surprise that takes our breath away and the joy that makes our body tingle. The body has its own emotional intelligence. It shows us what is going on inside us and how we feel, long before we have cognitively penetrated the sensation. It also stores emotions from the past, which then bubble to the surface in so-called trigger moments and sometimes call up an appropriate reaction to a scene from the past, but not from the present. Dealing with these triggers and patterns and questioning more closely why emotional reactions sometimes flare up so violently is an important part of self-study.

Inner leadership means recognizing these patterns and taking responsibility for them, so that ideally, it is not the private or professional environment that suffers from our trigger reaction, but a conscious handling of the inner state is possible. Sometimes it already helps to recognize and name the pattern when, for example,

---

[7] Brown, Brené: Atlas of the heart, New York 2021, p. 222.

a feeling of inadequacy threatens to turn into anger and to lash out in defense, where it is actually not necessary at all.

Especially in leadership positions, team members sometimeslack reflection on these patterns. I have often experienced as an employee, that I did not have the courage to address really exaggerated and unfair behavior by superiors. New Work approaches, such as flat hierarchies, a culture of error tolerance, and openness certainly create new spaces and opportunities for reflection that promote criticism and exchange—but the inner work on one's own emotional map remains, ultimately, an individual task.

Since I am already using the emotional map as an image here, it is worth noting, that some areas of this map remain unvisited. Especially in times of a never-ending smiling, perfect, happy flood of images that washes over our minds via social media, it can easily give the impression that everyone is always happy and worry-free. The term *Toxic Positivity* has been coined for this exclusion of supposedly negative emotions, which very aptly integrates the poisonous effect of suppressing feelings. Just because we don't allow them to be felt or think they don't suit us, doesn't mean they disappear. So in this chapter, I invite you to also visit those regions of the emotional map, that you may have avoided. I have discovered that where I least expected it, I found the most beautiful insights—able to transform old pain into acceptance, and integrate long-avoided sadness.

Wouldn't the world be boring if we were always just happy? And what is happiness without the other facets that we also know how to feel? Our spectrum of emotions, the inner rainbow of our feelings opens us to the world, to others and to life itself. And if these lines carry a touch of pathos, then let it be a sign of the emotional richness that lies dormant in all of us.

Reflection questions

The first question is obvious and you have been asked it at least as often as you probably ask others. What is often missing, though, is genuine, deep empathy with the answer.

1. How are you (really)? How am I (really)?
   I have the feeling that often the only desired answer to this is "great, and you?" At the same time, the most beautiful and intense conversations arise from this question when both sides are willing to open up and look more closely. "Great" or "Good" is said so quickly, an exchange is ended so quickly with it—and even if you are doing super well—what does that feel like exactly?
   To individually explore the inner emotional landscape, it helps to pay close attention to where emotions manifest physically.
2. Where and how do you feel certain emotions on a physical level?
   Describe the emotional sensitivity of your body, read the signs it gives you and take time to physically feel your emotions. Notice where you try to suppress or deny the body's reaction. Consciously visit the areas of your inner map that you rarely, if ever, visit.

3. What patterns of situational variables, experiences, and feelings do you know about yourself? Which patterns repeat themselves over and over again?
   It helps a lot to integrate trusted persons into the reflection. Often partners and friends start to avoid certain areas of your emotional life, to circumnavigate topics, to protect you (and themselves) from injuries. However, it is precisely these areas that want to be seen and understood, to be integrated into the map. Just because a pattern is avoided does not mean it is gone or healed. I am convinced that deep and loving relationships also have the task of recognizing, uncovering, and resolving these patterns mutually.
   Perhaps a situation comes to mind immediately, e.g., "Whenever I'm stuck in traffic, I get soooo angry!" Or "Whenever someone keeps me waiting, I feel sooo worthless." Or "Whenever I scroll through Instagram, envy rises in me."
   No "whenever" pattern is set in stone, it reflects something learned, and it can change. However, it usually does not do this on its own, but only through the corresponding willingness to reflect.

You are not your emotions

It often feels that way and we also speak that way: I am angry, I am sad, I am happy... Especially with feelings that are difficult for us to process or classify, it can be enormously helpful to take a first step back, gain distance and say "I feel sad" or "This makes me angry". This small shift contains an important change of perspective, a distance is restored, which makes it possible to look at the feeling more closely and to explore it, instead of being carried away by it.

This distancing is also essential in disputes with others, because once we have fallen into the vortex of our emotions and are strongly identified with them, the path to accusations of the other is not far: "I am angry because you..." A different formulation already allows more room for self-responsibility and dialogue: "It makes me angry when you... This is a pattern of mine, which is based on... Can you help me understand it better, overcome it, let it go?"

The way we deal with emotions, with inner patterns, the inner map of feelings, also plays a crucial role for the next chapter and topic.

Resilience

Like mindfulness, resilience has received growing attention in recent years.[1] It has gained popularity not only in scientific publications, but also across diverse platforms for knowledge sharing. There are several reasons for this. In the wake of the COVID-19 pandemic, many people long for more resilience or have at least found their psychological endurance tested daily. The climate catastrophe is already knocking at the door, anti-democratic tendencies are increasing worldwide, political hotspots are multiplying, and the modern work space introduces stressors and demands that push many people beyond their resilience limits.

I am not aiming to paint a bleak picture here, but rather to illustrate why the call for greater psychological resilience is growing louder. This includes the desire to prevent mental and psychological overload, burnout, and other exhaustion diseases, and to empower individual through resilience training. I find these approaches useful, but at the same time, I see the danger that offers to strengthen resilience are supposed to save us from external stress factors. It reflects a troubling mindset: We obverwork employees, but offer more resilience and mindfulness workshops as comensation. This is certainly not what I am trying to conceptualize with Mindful Leadership.

On the other hand, I find the outrtght rjection of practice-oriented resilience programs overly simplistic. Especially in university contexts, I have frequently encountered harsh criticism arguing that such "coaching" encourages neoliberal self-optimization and reinforces power dynamics. The fact that the structures of

[1] Wickert, N., Meents, A. Resilience—The inner resistance. Z Psychodrama Soziom19, 1–5 (2020). https://doi.org/10.1007/s11620-020-00523-7. Last accessed: 08.02.2022.

N. Plohr, *Mindful Leadership*, https://doi.org/10.1007/978-3-658-48300-5_11

the university often lead people to overextend themselves far beyond their limits, without ever receiving help or coaching, remains unspoken in this criticism.

So once again, it is my aim to find a middle ground and integrate resilience as part of Inner Leadership and Mindful Leadership, while also preserving the ability to criticize.

As implicitly described, resilience is defined as psychological resistance and the ability to be adaptable in difficult situations while remaining true to oneself. So resilience does not mean avoiding difficulties or never being confronted with stress. The resistance refers less to the stress itself than to the affective reaction to it. Thus, resilience is related to the conscious handling of emotions, indeed the reflection of emotional patterns, which was discussed in more detail in the last chapter, is already an exercise in resilience.

An example from a coaching session with a student shows the enormous effect that emotional reflection can have on our resilience. A student came to me with exam anxiety. In our first conversation, she told me why she would not pass the upcoming exam under any circumstances, what she was incapable of, how much fear she had of failure, and that she was already working through the nights, even though she was sure it would not help. I asked her the following questions in turn:

1. What past experiences have made your exam anxiety so strong? What fear lies behind the exam anxiety? **(Emotional patterns, Pattern)**
2. Why do you assume you will not pass the exam? Are there experiences that have already proven the opposite? (There were numerous, but in her subconscious only the one failed exam had stuck—we created a sober, number-based analysis and came up with an average of at least 35 passed to 1 failed exam. With this approach, my aim was to enable her to distance herself from her very emotional view of exams and also to help her develop a sense for her successes again. **Change of perspective, strengthen self-efficacy.**)
3. How did it feel to pass the 35 exams? What skills did you use to be successful over and over again? (Instead of picking up on her focus on her perceived weaknesses, I reminded her of her strengths and shifted her focus. It was noticeable how her entire body and also her voice relaxed more and more the longer she talked about her successes. **Give space to strengths, build self-confidence.**)
4. How can you prepare for the exam in a relaxed and efficient way at the same time? (Working through the nights put her nervous system under constant stress and fed her already large fears even more. We developed a schedule that also included fixed break times and took care of her physical and mental well-being. **Confront fear with clarity and organization. Strengthen physical and mental resources.**)
5. Would the world really end if you didn't pass? (She laughed. Was noticeably more relaxed than at the beginning of the conversation. **Restore relation. Learn to classify the task(s). Rediscover humor.**)

What is compressed here in a quick listing filled a three-hour coaching session in practice, with many tears, a few body exercises, and some detours.

However, the individual steps contain very basic information and inspirations for building resilience. Some basic building blocks are: self-efficacy, goal orientation, analytical ability, impulse control, joy of contact, and resource awareness. These key elements are not exhaustive, but emerge from the example. By joy of contact, I mean the courage that the student had to muster to approach me at all and to name and share her fear as such. I am sure you also know the phenomenon that stress always feels much bigger when you keep it to yourself and are alone with it. Especially in home office situations, overload is often not visible and emails continue to pile up, when perhaps a face-to-face conversation would better acknowledge already strained capacities of the employees.*

What becomes clear in the coaching example is that the resources are never just mental or psychological, but also physical in nature. It sometimes seems to me as if we still separate body and mind too consistently in approaches like resilience. However, mental and physical resilience are closely related. When physical resources are exhausted, the energy for conscious confrontation with emotional patterns is quickly lacking, the energy to focus on positive, strengthening thoughts is lacking, and sometimes absurdly also the energy to plan the next break. I often experience the latter in coaching contexts and workshops.

Rather than fostering a culture of regular breaks, I often hear sentences like: "Once we have finished the project, then we can take a pause." This calculation usually does not work out if the employees* exhaust themselves so much on the way to the completion of the project that they first completely fail, in order to be somewhat ready for action again at some point. How successfully changes are then really implemented, which were first shifted into the "If only first…" context, is probably known.

Resilience is not an acute emergency kit that comes into play when someone has an accident. It is a long-term and sustainably established practice that prevents exhaustion instead of compensating for it.

Therefore, it is best to practice resilience on a daily basis. As the above tagging already shows, there are many points to start from. Since I have already written a chapter on self-efficacy, the ability to analyze and impulse control plays a role in the emotions chapter and also appears in the example already described, I would like to focus once again on the topic of resources and in this context share an interpretation of resilience that I transfer to my coaching practice.

I often come up with ideas for my workshops and concepts by experimenting with the terms that concern me in their context. When I thought about the English word *resilience* and also about what constitutes strong mental resilience for me, I ended up with *resilience* as *recovery in silence*. What I mean by this is not the hermit-like silence that spreads when one largely withdraws from social life and meditates on enlightenment in a cave in the mountains, but an everyday, practical silence that can be sought again and again in between and unfolds as a familiar place of rest within.

I mean a silence that can be achieved with just one deep, conscious breath or with a fifteen-minute walk around the block (without a smartphone!) or with free writing at the beginning of a meeting. My feeling is that so many people are exhausted because there are often no islands of rest in the hustle and bustle of everyday life, the real silence. The so-called "radio silence", the "end of transmission" or even just the knowledge that a message will now be on its way to the recipient for a week and one will only have to deal with a reply then—all this has given way to a constant barrage of media, communication, entertainment, and information.

The yogis referred to the human mind as "Monkey Minds" in their first recorded writings. Jumping from branch to branch, always in motion, easily distracted, that was the intended analogy. What was true eight thousand years ago is today translated into technologies that so over-satisfy our mind's desire for entertainment and stimuli that it exhausts us.

Yoga originated from the idea of creating islands of rest for the mind. Meditation is the goal of yoga, the physical exercises on the way there are actually intended to prepare the body for the breathing exercises (Pranayama) and the long sitting in an upright meditation seat. The fact that the Western interpretation has translated yoga into movement-rich training sessions with twists, handstands, and a loud playlist, while meditation is broken off after three minutes so as not to bore the customers, pleases the Monkey Mind immensely, but largely misses the core of the original yogic thought.

Recovery in silence is therefore also not found in all yoga studios, where perhaps it is being sought. But the longing for silence is great. Anyone who has regularly taken the time to sit or lie down quietly once a day, to let their thoughts wander without clinging to them, will quickly have felt how grateful the body, the mind, the nervous system are for the much-needed break. You can call this meditation, but you don't have to. What happens when silence is allowed to enter is an active regeneration process of the entire body, but also of mental capacity. I always imagine how in a glass of water, in which sand is constantly being stirred up, peace finally sets in and each grain of sand slowly sinks to the bottom one by one, until the view into the glass is clear again.

This process strengthens both the physical and the psychological-mental defenses and, in my experience and that of many clients leads to ideas and creative processes start, which are not born out of necessity, but out of relaxation.

Above all, however, silence offers the thoughts and the entire system the opportunity to recover from the constant stimuli. Because there are often simply too many. Not all of them are necessary or meaningful. Anyone who (like me still often enough) catches themselves scrolling, checking the news for the fifteenth time, or listening to efficiency-driven podcasts during a walk in the "break", knows how often we flood ourselves with additional stimuli when we don't have to. Wanting to be entertained, sounded, and informed has now taken on addictive tendencies. This is not a media or technology apocalyptic view, but a correlation between constant media broadcasting and increasing states of exhaustion.

To consider resilience as recovery in silence therefore also means to actively create breaks, to seek and allow silence. Silence can initially feel very unfamiliar, even uncomfortable. Although there never seems to be enough time, in silence it suddenly becomes so present, so stretched, so available, that some people initially feel overwhelmed. But when the sand in the water glass settles, a delightful, wonderful silence sets in that strengthens and allows regeneration. And that is only too gladly sought again and again.123

Practical tips: Resilience as recovery in silence
To conclude this chapter in a practical way, I would like to provide some inspiration on how to integrate islands of peace and moments of silence into everyday life. I have already mentioned a few:

1. **Take a conscious, deep breath.** Especially in times when time seems to be running, it helps enormously to focus on your own breath and consciously slow it down and deepen it. When we are stressed, our breathing becomes shallow and superficial, which puts our stressed nervous system under even more tension. A vicious circle that can be broken by taking one (and preferably another) deep breath. Make sure you breathe into your stomach, this activates the diaphragm and contributes to stress reduction.
   Since you are breathing all day anyway, it makes a lot of sense to check in from time to time and ask yourself: How am I actually breathing? Relaxed and deep? Regenerative? Or stressed and shallow?
2. **Go for a walk without media distraction.** Just go for a walk. Without a podcast or music in your ears. Just walk. Breathe. Enjoy. Recharge your energy.
3. **Write a diary before going to bed.** Write down your thoughts, free the monkey mind from them and don't carry them into the night. So that real silence in your head is possible when you want to sleep.
4. **Also, sometimes don't talk.** At work, with friends, partners, family, also just take breaks from talking. I have developed a tool for teams for these days when you need more inner silence, which I introduce in part 2. But also in private contexts it is so important to be able to just be silent, to let the mind rest and to just be allowed to be.
5. **Grounding. Or also: just lie down.** The good old power nap really has its justification. I have an acquaintance who holds a leadership position for a large German company and regularly lies down in the middle of his office on the carpet, arms and legs slightly bent outstretched, palms facing upwards, eyes closed, breathing deeply into the stomach. Within a few minutes, the nervous system shuts down, the parasympathetic system is activated, as is the vagus nerve, which is responsible for the supply of all organs and our regeneration on many levels. At the beginning, his colleagues still laughed at him, but now there are many imitators and "grounding" has become an accepted resilience exercise in everyday office life.
6. **Mindful eating.** Who doesn't know it, the hasty, stressed, eating on the side in front of the laptop, smartphone or other media companions? If resilience

strengthening is mainly about replenishing and preserving your own resources, eating is a major energy supplier. But if stress is "eaten" instead of enjoyment and peace, you shouldn't be surprised after lunch break if you feel overfilled, burdened and exhausted. This can also occur if you gulp down the healthiest food in the world with a stressed mood in a noisy environment. Replacing so-called "stress eating" with conscious enjoyment can change a lot and support both the physical and psychological-mental immune system.

7. **Start the day with "nothing".** Call it meditation, call it conscious silence, call it what you like, but try it out. Get up a little earlier than usual, sit in an upright seat, close your eyes and let peace enter you. Feel the day rise before your inner eye and enjoy that you simply take time for yourself, for peace, for nothing, before everything else starts.

Creativity

I can remember well, or at least I think I do, how as a child I would sometimes walk to my parents with a drooping head and say, "I'm sooooo bored." Even before I could pronounce "bored" correctly, I was familiar with the feeling of time passing slowly, unfilled. And my parents' response also became a familiar one—"Really? But that's great, think of something new! Look, there you have… Look, the children over there, … Didn't you always want to…?" The parent trick worked, usually I found something I could craft, paint, or imagine. Or I approached other children, which as an only child always quickly helped me get over "boredom". The American sociologist Sherry Turkle aptly wrote about these moments: "Boredom is your imagination calling you."[1]

Nowadays I often enjoy the breaks from doing and creating and crafting, when time can stretch again, when a long while opens up. Boredom could actually be a welcome change in a world where so many conversations are accompanied by phrases like "Oh, if only I had more time" or "time flies" or "the day has too few hours". But I feel that most adults can bear it even less than children. Yet it is precisely from boredom, the long while, the gap, the pause, the "nothing", that so much creativity can emerge. Because finally there is time again to listen to the inner life, to listen to the ideas that are waiting for you, and to feel the courage rising within you to think beyond the beaten path once again. To do something new. Perhaps with a very specific goal, perhaps completely without one.

Creativity is the ability to create original things, to establish new connections, to develop new thoughts and to train a flexible mind that produces a wealth of ideas. This does not always have to manifest itself in works of genius, but can also find expression in creative solutions for a broken household appliance, or in the way one ties one's shoelaces or mounts a bicycle. Over the centuries, creativity

[1] Mindful Journal, Mindful Staff: 10.01.2016, https://www.mindful.org/smartphones-hurt-our-face-to-face-relationships-sherry-turkle/.

N. Plohr, *Mindful Leadership*, https://doi.org/10.1007/978-3-658-48300-5_12

has risen to become an attribute seemingly reserved only for particularly extraordinary people, yet we are all endowed with creative potential.

"Creativity is a ubiquitous phenomenon of human nature"[2] writes Joachim Funke, Professor of General Psychology. We are surrounded by various expressions of human creativity. Every building incorporates an architectural stroke, graffiti on house walls speak their own artistic language, every piece of clothing testifies to design-oriented thoughts and drafts, and even within us flows a stream of thoughts, sometimes more, sometimes less original, but always containing the potential to ignite a spark of ideas.

Again and again I meet people in coaching, at the university, in my circle of friends, who think that they are not creative. The author Elizabeth Gilbert disagrees: "If you are alive, you are a creative person"[3] she writes. If creativity is such a fundamental part of our humanity, then this topic naturally cannot be missing in this book on Inner and Mindful Leadership.

In work contexts, creativity is desired and often demanded under a certain time pressure. Time and creativity have a very unique relationship to each other, as the introductory quote from Sherry Turkle emphasizes. We can't always wait for boredom to enjoy our imaginative power. Generally, external pressure and creativity, as an energy directed from within, can be at odds. However, some types of creativity know how to convert the excitement of an approaching deadline into creative potential, and even need a certain pressure to transfer their creative power into practice. Others fall into freeze mode when a deadline approaches. Creativity follows individual rhythms.

Some find it easy and have the privilege of setting their own rhythm, others are overwhelmed by self-organization and oscillate between procrastination and overwork.

That procrastination, or "procrastinitis", is not always negative, but can even promote creativity, is conveyed by the psychologist and creativity researcher Nora Jacobs in her podcast Creativity x you.[4] She describes that a crucial phase of the creative process is the so-called incubation phase, in which the creative project is left lying and the thoughts can consciously be directed to something else. It is important that procrastination does not occur before starting the activity, but only once a start has been made, a first draft or an idea has taken shape.

The concept of "strategic procrastination" takes advantage of the subconscious continuation of work on a topic, which occurs even when we are not consciously thinking about certain problems. Not without reason do we use the saying: "I'll sleep on it," trusting that the unconscious phase of problem-solving can often lead

[2] Funke, Joachim: On the Psychology of Creativity, in: Dresler/Baudsen: Creativity. Contributions from the Natural and Humanities, Stuttgart 2008, p. 31.

[3] Gilbert, Elizabeth: Big Magic, New York 2015, p. 89.

[4] Podcast: Nora Jacobs: Creativity x you, Episode 2: What is creativity anyway? last accessed via Spotify: 04.03.2022.

to very clear ideas and results. Distracting oneself with other activities can also further promote creativity, according to Jacob. In particular, switching between activities that require high cognitive effort and those that demand less, such as washing dishes or hanging laundry, can be enormously helpful in stimulating creative performance. Switching between different creative projects can also work, especially when it can be freely decided when to dedicate oneself to which task.

If the creative flow of a project stalls, one turns to the other and directs energy into the task until a break is also announced here.

Nora Jacob recommends starting early and submitting late for projects that span a large period of time, to allow for phases of processing, leaving things be, and distraction, and to consider times of mental relief as part of creativity itself.[5] She repeatedly emphasizes that creativity cannot be reduced to a brief moment of idea, of inspiration, but follows a processual logic. The various phases of this process were already established by Wallas in 1926 and still hold a firm place in creativity research today. The five phases are:

1. Preparation: Collecting and searching for information and inspirations on the topic of the creation object
2. Incubation: Leaving the topic be, letting it rest, "mental incubation" and intuitive, subconscious concretization and bundling of the project
3. Insight: Flash of inspiration or intuition, aha effect, the moment of becoming aware of the creative momentum
4. Evaluation: Classification of creative enthusiasm into a more sober perspective with the question of the appropriateness and suitability of the idea
5. Elaboration: Getting into action and implementation

The fifth phase in particular harbors many pitfalls. So many wonderful ideas fizzle out in the concrete implementation. Here comes a characteristic of creativity that might be surprising at first. Discipline.

In interviews with writers, painters, creatives, I encounter it again and again: Without discipline and a structured workday, no creative processes get started—and above all, they are not brought to a conclusion. In this respect, creativity is also tied to habit formation, which sets up regular time blocks for creative work in the daily routine. Creativity can, according to Nora Jacobs, actually be "practiced" in this way and, as with all other practices, developed as a skill through routine repetition and fixed times. This may give hope especially to those who would not describe themselves as creative, but would like to be.

Creativity requires courage, Nora Jacobs also emphasizes this in her podcast and refers, among other things, to Brené Brown, who names courage as one of the main characteristics of successful leaders.[6] This touches on a paradox that again

---

[5] Ibid.

[6] Podcast: Nora Jacobs: Creativity x you, Episode 34: How much courage does creativity need?, last accessed via Spotify: 04.03.2022.

emerges when considering the media penetration of our present. While creativity is explicitly desired, even demanded, and is also named by large companies as one of the most important characteristics of executives and employees, it is still risky to present oneself and share creative ideas that do not conform to the norm.

Thinking differently, thinking creatively is indeed desired, but still always within a clearly defined framework of conformity. Testing the limits of creative obstinacy begins already in school, where conformity is usually graded better than creativity. This is mainly due to the fact that the latter, despite various test formats, is difficult to measure and is not always conducive to peace and order in the classroom. The boundaries of what can be said and done are negotiated every second in social media. Interestingly, platforms that encourage self-expression and sharing lead on the one hand to high diversity—but on the other hand also to normative and often enough judging tendencies, which do not always appear inviting and creativity-promoting. Is it surprising that in the absence of a culture of error, in strong evaluation and condemnation tendencies, an economy of likes and dislikes, the creative thoughts do not immediately bubble up?

Creativity requires unconventional, cheeky, flexible, playful, courageous thinking. And thus a space, a framework, in which mistakes are allowed. Sometimes creativity is not inhibited by external expectations and demands, but by internal critics. Perfectionism is, as Elizabeth Gilbert puts it, "fear in high heels"[7]—fear that is chicly packaged, but still implies fear of failure. Therefore, it is not only important to establish an external framework in which creative work and "making mistakes" are allowed, but also to develop an internal attitude that allows oneself to try out new things without having to achieve perfect results immediately.

In order to get into action after the phases of collecting, letting rest, and concretizing, it can be enormously helpful to create a setting that promotes individual creativity. The habitualization of creative processes can, for example, start with choosing a playlist that is always played when you immerse yourself in your project. The spatial setting also plays a big role. Those who prefer silence and solitude to fully devote themselves to creation need a retreat and the certainty of being undisturbed. Those who find silence too loud may prefer a co-working café, an open-plan office, or a park. It is worth trying out what promotes your own creative process, what stimulates thoughts without overwhelming them. To this day, I like the mix of writing at home, which I usually prefer in the morning when the day is still quiet and it is slowly getting light, and writing in a café, in the afternoon, amidst other busy people balancing their laptops on their knees and sipping cappuccino or having conversations with their companions.

The first setting allows me to dive deep into the text, the second is more like a light-footed being in the middle. The café allows me to listen to the noise and filter

[7] Gilbert, Elizabeth: Big Magic, New York 2015, p. 165.

out individual snippets from it, which then perhaps stimulate words and sentences that flow directly into the keys.

Not only the change of projects and topics, but also the change of creative settings can be enormously helpful and a lot of fun.

I would like to mention one last point before I come to the final reflection questions. Speaking of fun.

Elizabeth Gilbert emphasizes in her book "Big Magic" again and again that creativity does not necessarily have to go hand in hand with an artistic self-hatred or a kind of transfigured martyrdom.[8] She criticizes the stylization of artistic suffering and advocates giving creativity back its playful curiosity and allowing oneself to feel joy in creative work. I was promptly reminded of the scientific habitus, which taught me again and again during my doctoral time that it must be a rocky, difficult path to the submission of the dissertation. Which led to me almost feeling strange or wrong when it once felt "light-footed". Over time, I adapted and became almost suspicious when sentences "just like that" flowed from my pen, because these could not really be intellectual enough if they gave me intuitive joy. Interestingly, I only found my way back to the laptop and the process of writing when I reclaimed the joy of it and managed to block out the pressure and evaluation criteria for a while.

Elisabeth Gilbert describes a similar, almost defiant joy in writing, which was not impressed by numerous rejections from publishers and magazines in her inbox.

Why should creativity have to go hand in hand with suffering? What is better about intellectual work if it makes you feel miserable and inferior? Creativity can be fun, bring joy, be light-footed and release energies. Maya Angelou once said: *"You can't use up creativity. The more you use, the more you have."*[9] So why not risk it and just give it a try?

Creativity tools and inspirations

- Become aware of where in your everyday life you are already creative. Creativity is not only found in great works, but also in small practices. Perhaps you are creative in the way you arrange and select flowers, in note-taking, or in trying out new cooking recipes. No matter how small your creative impulses seem to you, take the time to make them conscious.
- You can take this reflection even further and write a creativity CV. In which phases of your life were you particularly creative? How old were you? What did you do and how did you feel about it?
- Practice strategic procrastination. As now scientifically substantiated, the phase of letting go and putting aside projects is even beneficial to the creativity

[8] Gilbert, Elizabeth: Big Magic, New York 2015, p. 212.

[9] Maya Angelou, quoted in: Neil Pavitt: Brainhack: Tips and Tricks to unleash your brain's full potential, UK/Cornwall 2016, p. 115.

process. Likewise, switching between projects at your own pace. So: Give it a try!

- Create a creative routine. Regularly make time and space to let your creativity run free. You've always wanted to…? Let's go.
- Explore your own creativity. What do you need to really get into the flow? Silence? Bustle? Voices? Music? Walks? What times suit you to create? The morning? The evening? (I advise against the night, I think it's another characteristic of a false artistic attitude, not needing daylight and sleep…)
- If you can't make progress in a creative process or are chewing on a problem in vain, change the medium. Paint your bachelor's thesis, visualize individual chapters e.g. using building blocks or glasses, give a project and its subcategories colors or fantasy names, package a problem into a story, create a "vision board", a collage, talk to a friend about a project she has no background information or expertise on. All these examples lead to a change of perspective that can get your perhaps frozen thought patterns moving again.
- Move. Often the best ideas come while walking, jogging—in any case, physical movement helps to set thoughts in motion as well. Involve your whole body in the creative process.
- Change the creative setting. Sometimes it helps just to change the side of the desk to get a new perspective. Sometimes the sparks of ideas are waiting in the café around the corner or in the office of colleagues, the apartment of a friend. Find places where you feel comfortable and inspired.
- If you feel like you're not creative, have no idea and are waiting in vain for the "spark", ask yourself: What am I interested in? Interest is a door to intrinsic motivation, to an interest in topics/things/projects guided from inside to outside. Your interest, your intrinsic motivation, is highly likely to lead you into your creative ability.
- What prejudices about creativity might still be in your way? That it is reserved only for the chosen ones? That it must go hand in hand with creative suffering? That it needs a lot of attention from an audience? Write them all down and take another close look. Maybe it's time to say goodbye to them.
- Gather all your courage and start.

The way we live and navigate our lives, constantly requires creativity. We adapt, search for solutions to problems and settings that life offers us, are challenged to steer what we have learned into new paths and to link it differently than habit dictates. The more courage we develop to approach tasks creatively, the more ideas flow. This creative mindset is again not reserved for a special group of people, but can be learned by each individual in their own way.

Between control and surrender, discipline and break, routine and novelty, trust and search, there is a chance that over time a "sweet spot" of creativity will emerge, a state in which everything flows, becomes effortless and light. A state of complete presence and happiness, a state so fulfilling that any externally guided purpose of doing fades into the background.

Part II
Mindful Leadership

Before proceeding with the second part of this book and incorporating the results of interviews and further research in the following chapters, I would like to invite you to take a brief pause and try out the Mindful Breathing Technique by Thich Nhat Hanh. The power of consciously using your breath, continually returning to breathing when the present seems to slip away, is an essential component of mindfulness practice and can be practiced right up to your last breath.

Breathing connects the inside and outside, making it a wonderful transition between the two parts of this book and the practices they describe. Both in the quiet reflection of inner needs, emotions, and experiences, as well as in moments of communication and co-creation with others, conscious breathing is a key to presence, mindfulness, and creativity.Mindful Breathing Technique

Like so many Zen Buddhist masters, Thich Nhat Hanh uses simple words and instructions to invite us into the miracle of mindfulness and presence. It is a simplicity in which all complexity remains contained. It testifies to simple beauty and wisdom and is an invitation to all who have the courage to pause for a moment and direct their attention to the breath by incorporating the following sentences.

"Breathing in, I enjoy my in-breath."

Exhaling, I enjoy my out-breath.

When I breathe in, my entire body harmonizes with the inhalation.

Exhaling, my entire body is in harmony with the out-breath.

As I inhale, my entire body savors the tranquility of my in-breath.

When exhaling, my entire body enjoys the relaxation of my out-breath.

Breathing in, I enjoy the harmony of my in-breath.

Exhaling, I enjoy the harmony of my out-breath."[1]

Thich Nath Hanh adds: "Breathing like this is mindfulness, and as you sustain mindfulness, that is concentration. Wherever there is concentration, there is insight—a breakthrough—bringing more peace, understanding, love and joy into your life."[2]

---

[1] Thich Nath Hanh: The Art of living, New York 2017, p. 10.

[2] Ibid.

Mindfulness is a lifelong practice that, similar to the breath, often eludes our consciousness. And yet, from the simple act of inhaling and exhaling, a whole chain of effects emanates. Effects inward, into our bodies and streams of thought, but also outward, into the words we speak, the movements we make, the encounters and spaces we shape together with others.

Mindful Leadership accordingly begins with turning towards breathing, not only at the beginning of this chapter, but continuously, over and over again. Pleasurable in, relaxed out.

The harmony that we establish within ourselves through conscious breathing, we also carry into the world—into offices and lecture halls, into conference rooms and cafes, into public transport and studios. Wherever we breathe, we radiate our energy and our presence.

Mindful Leadership is associated on many levels with the ability to be present, to fully arrive in the moment, and to assign a place to both the past and the present within it. Especially in times of increasing digitalization, the ability to be present, to concentrate, and to organize distraction scenarios is an ongoing challenge. Particularly in times of change, when high flexibility, mental agility and creativity, are demanded from all team members, the presence of body and mind is a basic prerequisite. "Wherever there is concentration, there is insight"[3], says Thich Nhat Hanh. Concentration, presence, and mindfulness are closely intertwined. They are an essential part of the practice of Mindful Leadership and form the foundation for everything else. Just as breathing enables everything else and yet is so often forgotten, turning towards the present moment is the prerequisite for all future-oriented creation and vision.

Methodological Framework for Part II

Not only to guide into this second part on a meta-level, but also very pragmatically, method-oriented, here are a few sentences about the chosen approach and the collection of data material.

In addition to observations, literature research, and narratives, I weave quotes from interviews into the following chapters to offer a greater diversity of perspectives and to place the question "What is Mindful Leadership?" in a broader context. These are qualitative interviews that I conducted using open-ended questions whenever possible to allow for a high diversity of responses. The interviewees work in different industries and are only partially familiar with mindfulness practices. In this process, I primarily, but not exclusively, interviewed people in leadership positions to also pursue the initially mentioned hypothesis that every person, regardless of their position within the company, can develop leadership qualities.

In the discussions, my aim was to jointly explore and gauge what Mindful Leadership means to the interviewees and what they associate with the practice of mindful leadership work.

As a first result, I would like to note at this point that some of the keywords that were mentioned, despite all industry-specific differences, were very similar. The

[3] Ibid.

ones particularly strongly represented were: responsibility, communication, empathy, openness, error culture, creativity, courage, belonging, and recognition.

In describing and classifying the terms and corresponding practices, there was often a switch between the inner and outer dimension. There was often an awareness of the impact of the inner attitude on external conflicts or situations, but this was expressed very differently in the conversations and was also managed in everyday work using a variety of strategies. It was also noticeable that most managers did not receive specific coaching or internal training before they moved into the management position. Most described a "jump into the deep end", as a result of which they developed a certain attitude and an individual style themselves.

Coaching was most often only used when simmering conflicts or tangible problems had already arisen. Often, the reflection of daily interaction simply falls victim to the overwhelming daily business. Teams tend to react to changing dynamics and settings rather than actively and co-creatively, more from the outside in, than from the inside out.

I sincerely hope that this book and the workshop formats built upon it can contribute to initiating the reflection process, engaging in dialogue, and courageously asking: What is Mindful Leadership for me/us?

Flow

"Your concentration is complete. Your thoughts do not wander. You think of nothing else: You are totally absorbed in what you are doing…The energy flows very easily. You feel relaxed, pleasant, and energetic."[1] These words come from a dancer who Mihaly Csikszentmihalyi interviewed in the course of his flow research. I particularly like this quote because the language itself reflects the ease of the flow state. And at the same time, it becomes clear that the flow of energy also requires investment and concentration. Flow only occurs when energy is given clear direction and is allowed to fully unfold in an activity. What sounds so light-footed in the dancer's words has become a challenge, especially in a media environment of constant potential distractions. Fortunately, overcoming difficulties is itself part of the flow process, so dealing with media can also produce new forms of flow.

It was not initially planned to end this first part of the book with "Flow", but the longer I write this text, the clearer it becomes to me that leadership, in the best case, leads to flow experiences—for oneself, but also for the environment in which one moves, works, and has an impact. Again, the path leads from inside to outside, from the individual exploration of one's own flow experiences to what supports groups and teams in immersing themselves in the flow.

Mihaly Csikszentmihalyi repeatedly emphasizes that there can be no general recipe for flow (and thus also for happiness and deep joy of life), but the most diverse activities contain the potential for flow experiences. Whether playing chess, writing, dancing, or gardening: In the ideal state, energy flows easily and all limiting circumstances and worries recede into the background during the activity, the sense of time fades, a state of effortless joy sets in.

---

[1] Csikzentmihalyi, Mihaly: Flow. The Secret of Happiness, Stuttgart 1992, p. 93.

N. Plohr, *Mindful Leadership*, https://doi.org/10.1007/978-3-658-48300-5_13

In his book "Flow and Creativity," Mihaly Csikszentmihalyi succinctly presents the nine main elements of flow, which I would like to mention and briefly explain here.

1. Each phase of the process is characterized by clear goals.
   This point describes not only a predetermined goals, but also a clear sense of what to do next. In the act itself, one step follows from the next.
2. One receives immediate feedback for one's own actions.
   Be it the brushstroke on the canvas, the dancing step, the sound of the violin, or the written sentence—flow needs the feedback that reflects the joy of doing.
3. Tasks and abilities are in balance.
   Under-challenge is as disruptive to flow as over-challenge—the tingling feeling of being able to cope with a task is the best prerequisite for flow.
4. Action and awareness form a unity.
   Here there is a kinship to mindfulness as targeted attention involving all the senses and a presence in the moment. If attention is not fully dedicated to the present action and moment, no flow is possible.
5. Distractions are excluded from flow consciousness.
   If one manages to focus attention and immerse oneself in an activity, all everyday worries fall away, all (internal and external) distractions become irrelevant.
6. One has no fear of failure.
   Even the fear of failing or not being enough recedes in the flow and gives way to the flowing action. There is no room for fear, joy fills everything.
7. Self-forgetfulness.
   To describe it in the terms of this book: People pleasing falls away. All external orientation and doubts about how others might evaluate one's own actions are simply irrelevant in the flow. The ego has no desire to protect itself. Mihaly Csikszentmihalyi writes: *"After a flow experience, the self-concept is usually strengthened. [...] Paradoxically, the self grows through acts of self-forgetfulness."*[2]
   This self-forgetfulness allows space for expression and the joy of creating. The sense of self is absorbed in the action and is contained in it at the same time. At the same time, the often limiting questions and doubts of an externally oriented, socially framed self fall away, and the core, the joy of being oneself, have free rein.
8. The sense of time is suspended.
   Hours pass like minutes, experienced time takes precedence over measured time, and it doesn't really matter how long something takes because the action suspends any sense of time.

[2] Csikszentmihalyi, Mihaly: Flow and Creativity, Stuttgart 1997, p. 165.

9. The activity becomes autotelic.
   It pursues no external purpose, but is an end in itself because it brings joy and enables the state of flow. This leads back to the first point, because the goal setting is already aimed at creating, at the action itself, and not at another, externally oriented purpose, such as generating money or recognition. This does not mean that a paid activity cannot also be transformed into a flow activity.

This last point contains a critical component that Mihaly Csikszentmihalyi also addresses. If activities are only taken up for autotelic reasons and because they bring joy, the accusation of egocentrism can quickly arise.

Therefore, it is important to note that Mihaly Csikszentmihalyi does not only relate the flow experience to the self and its strengthening, but also emphasizes the integration of what has been learned, which is essentially in sharing the experiences and insights that have been gained. Anyone who always indulges in self-gratifying action will probably hit the limits of joy on their own, as we are dependent on the social component of our creation and are constantly reminded to make the added value of our actions accessible to others.

Turning towards one's own and individual flow experiences is not egocentric, but concentrated. If concentration and immersion in an activity are successful, the self is enhanced and strengthened in its complexity and can subsequently contribute more to an integrated context in community with others.

Turning towards oneself is therefore a prerequisite for interacting with others and becoming creative together. I emphasize this so strongly here because I repeatedly notice in my work with executives how difficult it can be to shift the focus inward and not be swept away by external circumstances and urgencies.

The "purposeless" flow activities or creative tasks that bring joy are often the first to be rationalized away and must give way to the loud to-dos. Especially in the flow moments, which do not always have to be directly related to work, there is often exactly the energy, joy, and creativity that is so urgently needed. Similar to the topic of creativity, the search for flow also involves setting up time and space to be able to immerse oneself in this state at all. Flow itself cannot be planned or calculated, but the time windows to devote oneself to activities and settings that enable flow can be. My observation is that the long-term effects of flow experiences on all areas of activity and general well-being are often underestimated to such an extent that everything that initially seems "purposeless" is lost sight of. But if one takes seriously the strengthening of self-esteem, which Mihaly Csikszentmihalyi describes as a result of flow, this affects all areas of life and work. A stronger sense of self is associated with better decision-making and differentiation skills, more empathy and capacity for the concerns of others, and a high degree of trust in one's own abilities, which also leads to a smoother and more efficient flow of energy outside of the flow state.

This chapter is therefore once again an invitation to review your own priority list and dare to give more time and space to the joy of creating.

Another point that fascinates me about flow is the relationship between control and trust. Because even though the feeling of having everything under control sets in during flow, this is not the case when viewed rationally. Following my own horizon of experience, I always have to think directly of skiing, which for me is an absolute flow activity. If you look at the movement sequence of skiing, it is always the combination of letting glide and applying pressure to the ski, tension and relaxation, holding on and letting go, that makes the movement succeed. The skis draw a track in the slope and at the same time the mountain, the snow speaks its own language. In flow, these elements come together, the body reacts, but also merges, with the ski, with the snow, and everything becomes light.

This touches on a physical component of flow, which is confirmed in the experience reports and interviews that Mihaly Csikszentmihalyi cites. Flow is not just a state of the head or mind (even though mental activities can lead to flow), but affects every cell of the body and is a bodily experience of presence, alignment, and energy flow. The joy that sets in during flow is not just a mental one, but a holistic, body-energizing joy.

Even though flow itself is a state of easy flowing and enables the realization of being this flow, the activities that lead to flow are quite strenuous. Especially the path towards balancing control and letting go leads not only in skiing to crash landings, frustrations and new attempts. Flow does not occur when a task is too easy, but when our collected concentration and presence is required. Flow and discipline do not contradict each other, but mutually promote each other. Often, many hours of practice precede the light-footed creation, movement, or action. Discipline is also required to repeatedly take time and space for the flow activity and to communicate its equal relevance to everyday tasks. The flow-induced dissolution of time and space perception is preceded by an organization of time and space.

As a media scientist, I am interested in this context in how digital media and media behavior affect flow experiences. Here, the role of media is ambivalent, as in so many other contexts.

Playing computer games, for example, can lead to flow states. When I was allowed to give a workshop on sports mental training at the E-Sports team of Holstein Kiel, I did not need to explain what flow is. The eyes lit up, everyone knew. They described the direct merging with the console, the immediate transmission of the sent signals to the avatars, but also the flow of the game, the anticipation of game moves and the complete presence in the game action.

Also, the use of digital devices for writing, moving, designing, painting, and communicating is not a hindrance to flow, but can promote it when used intentionally. When I think of the tedious typing, correcting, and handling of the typewriter, digital writing programs certainly bring some conveniences. It can promote flow to be able to simply delete or overwrite sentences, try out different fonts, and let the fingers glide over the smooth keyboard surface. But I also know writers who consciously reach for analog devices, rediscover the typewriter, and dive into the flow through the sound of the keys, the haptics of the surfaces, and the very own rhythm of writing.

What media, whether analog or digital, bring with them is a familiarity and rhythmization of the creative process. For example, if I take my laptop to a café and open it in a new place, the view that the display reflects to me is still the same.

This may seem banal, but it is important for the process of creating. Flow, like creativity, needs a certain routine, a reliable framework that can then be filled with free flow.

In addition to rhythmization through media, they can also cause permanent interruptions. Digital media in particular harbor such a large variety of distraction scenarios that these too must be "organized" in order not to constantly prevent the experience of flow.

If all mailboxes and addressing options are kept open, we are permanently on alert and expecting interruptions, even if no messages arrive. As the introductory quote makes clear, flow requires our full concentration, not the half, distributed, constantly distracted version of our abilities. The conscious switching between projects and activities does not hinder creativity or flow, but being permanently interrupted (potentially) does.

The latter has a negative effect on our concentration performance, but also on our psychological and mental health. Experiencing flow is a holistic sensation of joy and self-efficacy and has a significant influence on our self-confidence and self-esteem. If this energy flow is constantly disrupted and prevented, over time the moments of recharging, of letting go, even of happiness, are missing. This happiness, this deep joy, cannot be replaced by pleasure and quick dopamine kicks as enabled by social media, for example. Mindless scrolling on Instagram may seem entertaining at first glance, but it does not bring about real, deep joy. The content is predetermined, many short visual stimuli are presented to us, at best dopamine is released briefly or a moment of inspiration is enabled. Often enough, however, the platform leaves one feeling somewhat joyless and empty.

Media can thus both promote and inhibit flow, depending on how we use them. The conscious and goal-oriented use of media instead of a consumption-led passive reception is one of the most important prerequisites for immersing oneself in the flow with them.

In conclusion, I would like to note that flow—like creativity—follows its own rhythm. We are not made to be in flow all the time, but need the contrast, the break, the other. Flow releases energy, but also requires our physical and mental resources. If we were always and everywhere in flow, we could not distinguish it as a particularly happiness-promoting state. The integration of the experienced would also be neglected, the differentiation of the created, as well as the sharing with others. So we also need breaks from letting go, in which we replenish our resources and have other experiences. Flow cannot be forced. Flow needs trust. And devotion. To the joy when it occurs, but also to the serenity when it evaporates again.

Reflection questions

1. When were you last in flow? How did the state feel, what was right in your environment so that you could really dive in? What are flow activities for you?
2. Is there a certain music that leads you into the state of energy flow? A smell? A place where you feel inspired?

3. How do you keep yourself from flow experiences? Do you let your attention scatter, what always distracts you? How can you organize distraction scenarios, mute, hide, to allow yourself the flow?
4. Do you tend towards perfectionism? What if it didn't matter at all what comes out of your actions and how others find it?
5. Do you sometimes get stuck in "if I first...then" loops? As if you always had to earn the things that just "only" bring you joy? How about reversing your priorities and starting every day with what brings you joy and does not pursue an external purpose? And even if it's only three minutes, how would that feel? How much time that you think you can't invest in your flow activities do you spend on "empty pleasure" that, if you're honest, actually bores you?
6. Do you perceive your media use as more flow-promoting or inhibiting? What can you change?
7. What activities would you pursue even if no one paid you for them, no one applauded you for them, no one even knew you were doing them? What do you do just for pure joy?

And so this chapter literally ends with pure joy and, beyond that, with a final quote from Mihaly Csikszentmihalyi, which hopefully not only invites reflection, but also the implementation of inspirations for the practice of *Inner Leadership*: "It is not enough to *know* how to do it, one must *do* it [...]"[3]

[3] Csikszentmihalyi, Mihaly: Flow. The Secret of Happiness, Stuttgart 1992, p. 45.

(Meta-)Communication

A babble of voices fills the seminar room. My students are engrossed in an exercise that I explained to them a short while ago. In groups of three, they each take on the speaking, listening, or observing role and note down their findings. Before we dive into practice, I always begin by collecting all the points that they associate with "successful communication".

Often one of the first responses is: "Listening well." Or also "That exactly what is said is understood." And then it often becomes easier to describe what all is involved: "Empathy." "Presence." "Body language must match." Usually, even before the exercise, a colorful chalkboard picture emerges, which is supplemented after the exercise. Most are initially surprised at how much they "overhear", "do not remember", "shorten", "omit". The task includes the listening part involves repeating the counterpart's narration and staying as close as possible to the tone and tonus of the narrative. Some observers find that the listening and repeating part begins with the emotions, others tell much more on the factual level or even completely disregard the emotionality.

The practical exercise results in that by the end of an approximately thirty-minute unit, we have laid most of the foundations for communication models, which are then presented in the following. This directly refers to the experience and can be more easily abstracted from practice, because the communication situation was experienced and not just theoretically discussed.

Although all my interview partners agreed on the relevance of communication processes for their company and, funnily enough, often literally picked up the initially quoted sentence "Communication is the be-all and end-all", in the vast majority of cases it unclear what this "be-all and end-all" specifically meant.

N. H. is 28 years old and, together with two other executives, leads a team of a total of 80 employees at Deutsche Bahn Netze in Hamburg. In conversation with him, it became clear how important communication with the employees is to him. Several times in our conversation he emphasized his "[…] always open door." He

N. Plohr, *Mindful Leadership*, https://doi.org/10.1007/978-3-658-48300-5_14

reads a lot about leadership in his free time and continues his education, but he does not receive any coaching in the company itself and has not been specifically prepared for his role as a manager. When asked whether there were formats within the team in which internal communication were addressed, he replies: "No, I find that somehow artificial. With us, it develops more organically. It is important to me that everyone knows that they can talk to me at any time."

That communication is not explicitly adressed, although it is the be-all and end-all, as is always emphasized, is not uncommon.

Again and again, I receive requests for coaching with the request to do "something on the topic of communication", recently an HR person said on the phone: "Communication is always good. Can you do something about it?"

As a coach, of course, I appreciate the freedom these requests offer, but they also show that in day-to-day business there is often no time to go to the meta-level and reflect on communication processes.

To give space. As with so many very basic practices of our social interaction, these often fall out of focus. Similar to a pair of glasses, which, due to their daily use, are no longer perceived, the same applies to language as a means of communication. How communication is carried out in a company can usually be best observed by new employees, as they still have to acquire the internal language, rhythms of interaction, perhaps even company-specific vocabulary, which for all others have long since felt "completely normal" and therefore difficult to focus on.

Belonging is formed through language, it provides the framework for communication, in the best case it opens spaces for encounter and reflection inward and outward. In order to express oneself in a certain way, to engage in exchange, yes, even to be able to classify emotions and situations, a linguistic framework is needed, sometimes also specific vocabulary and moderations that make it possible to translate conflicts, recognition and the whole muddle of human encounters into a form of communication.

If all this does not happen and there is no organic coexistence and openness in the team, as N. H. describes and which is significantly linked to his own ability to reflect as a manager, there is a risk that the uncertainty due to unclear communication from the management level will spread into whispering and rumor spreading in the digital and analog corridors. This is described by C. P., former manager in a hotel, where she resigned shortly before our conversation, among other things, because *"[…] a lot was wrong with the communication."*

She herself worked most of the time in the home office: "We had no meta-level, no meetings or rules for communication, especially for me in the home office that was super difficult. I always said, please write everything down, so that we are all on the same page. I often did not feel a sense of belonging because I was only on site one day and then had so much information missing."

She describes that there was an internal tool to record regular updates important for the entire team. However, this tool was used less and less over time, leading to ever-growing information gaps among employees. She adds, "There simply need to be certain guidelines for communication, who to whom, what… Often I sat in some meetings and didn't know exactly why, so I think more meetings wouldn't have been the solution, but more clarity, who, why, what for. The better you communicate, the fewer meetings you need."

I can share this observation. If communication paths are clearly drawn and a meeting culture is established that aligns with openly communicated goals, there is no need for hours-long sessions that tire all participants. Then short check-ins for content update are sufficient and subsequently more time remains for encounters on a human, personal level. The uncertainty and lack of clarity in communication "from the top" continued, according to C. P., throughout the entire team and led to a shift in mood and experiences of frustration arising from general disorientation. An internal communication problem subsequently also became an external one, as the mood affected "the entire house" and thus also the hotel's external image.

From the small interview excerpts and paraphrases, the following can already be deduced:

1. Successful communication requires a clear structure that also offers flexibility.
2. Meetings are only effective if they pursue a clear goal and everyone is aware of why they are participating. It is helpful to continually question whether a particular meeting format is still needed or whether it may need to be revised or abolished.
3. Communication is closely intertwined with the feeling of belonging.
4. The time spent on meta-structuring communication processes ultimately results in immense time (and nerve) savings in daily exchange.

Not only for communication in everyday business, but also in specific conflict situations, it is very helpful if a certain framework is provided that clarifies the basis for discussion.

Joana Breidenbach and Bettina Rollow share in their book New Work needs Inner Work an "escalation ladder" of conflict situations, which I would like to include and classify in the context of this book. They define the following four stages in their practice-tested model:

1. I seek clarification in myself.
2. I seek clarification with you.
3. We agree on a mediator.
4. We agree on a decision-maker.[1]

At the first escalation level, and for clarification with oneself, it can be very helpful to turn to the inner storytellers, which were already described in the first part of this book. The reflection questions at the end of the chapter can also contribute to clarification at the first escalation level.

[1] Breidenbach, Joana/Rollow, Bettina: New Work needs Inner Work, Munich 2019, p. 118 f.

The confrontation with the inner conflict becomes more concrete when another reflection approach by Brené Brown is added at this point.

She summarizes the inner escalation, which can already be triggered by small cues, as "the story I'm making up".[2] As already described in the first part, the inner stories we tell ourselves are not always truthful. We invent them, we *make* them, create them, often based on past experiences and for our own protection.

The story that is told on the basis of a conflict is often not the one that corresponds to reality, but the one that reinforces our self-image and worldview. If we turn to the "story" that we derive from the conflict at the first escalation level, we can more easily take responsibility and ask ourselves: Where does this story come from that I am telling myself? Is it one that I have dug up from the past? What can I learn from this story about myself? And in a second step: What does the "story I'm making up" teach me about the other person and the relationship we maintain? Is the solution to the conflict perhaps already in the story itself? Is it even necessary to let the other person in on it?

If this can be denied, the conflict has already been resolved and the direct conversation is not even needed. If not, then the conflict is at escalation level two.

However, confrontation is not approached unprepared or impulsively, but rather with insights gained through inner introspection and assumption of responsibility. In the best case, all team members are familiar with the concept of escalation levels and also the principle of the "Story, I'm making up".

A company I have worked with several times has shortened Brené Brown's approach to "SIMU" (**S**tory **I**'m **M**aking **U**p). If a conflict arises based on an inner story, team members approach one another using the term "SIMU" as a reference point. This way, all involved team members already know that the person who feels the conflict within themselves has caught on to the "SIMU" and is now asking the others for help and further assessments. This directly enables a more open exchange that, instead of leading to confrontation, accusations and escalation, focuses on joint clarification and reflection. The prerequisite is that all team members know about "SIMU" and bring with them a willingness for self-reflection and personal responsibility.

Even level three of a conflict is much easier to implement if all team members are informed about the escalation model and its application. If a third person is involved, they can directly ask: Level 3 or 4? and thereby know what role they are expected to play in the conflict. If they are merely moderating at the third level, decision-making power is transferred to them at the fourth level.

Both approaches presented provide a clear framework for very individual conflict situations and at the same time call for personal responsibility. If all team members agree on the corresponding procedure, they are also given the freedom to resolve conflicts among themselves and to select moderators and decision-makers who they consider suitable for the specific situation. Instead of carrying

---

[2] Brown, Brené: Rising strong, London 2015, p. 86.

every conflict directly to the outside, the model always first leads inward, into self-reflection.

This requires a certain level of maturity and a willingness to turn the focus inward and to deal with oneself. Joana Breidenbach and Bettina Rollow repeatedly emphasize that this form of collaboration does not suit all people equally. In this context, they also count as conflict maturity, "[...] to acknowledge that some differences simply cannot be resolved."[3]

Another very practical tool to distribute the responsibility for communication across the entire team and to symbolize specific tasks for a meta-perspective on communication processes is a playful element that I call Me Viewer/Team Viewer.

The "Me Viewer" consciously directs attention during a meeting or even throughout an entire day inward, to oneself. The "only task" of the Me Viewer is to observe oneself, to reflect, to take notes and to write down questions that arise during the day or meeting. The Me Viewer has permission to completely withdraw from ongoing team conversations and discussions, but can also participate if both directions of attention, inward and outward, can be maintained simultaneously.

The idea behind playing the Me Viewer card, which can actually be used as a physical card or game piece in presence meetings, is that in this way self-reflection is given an active and clearly communicated part in everyday business life. If all team members know the meaning of the card, it is not strange or irritating if the playing person withdraws more, is quieter and occupied with themselves. Who doesn't know those days when exactly that would be "due", but involvement in external processes and dynamics leaves no room for reflection? The Me-Viewer card is a means to integrate self-reflection as a technique into everyday business life. Without having to explain themselves, the card can be played and everyone else knows. The card serves to observe one's own role behavior within a team, perhaps to catch a SIMU or to take a new position within the team.

The second card, the Team-Viewer, is used when a meta-perspective on team communication, as well as on the mood and creativity of the team, is needed. Instead of devoting attention to the contents of meetings and projects, the Team Viewer observes the dynamics in the team and asks themselves, for example: How is the team doing? How efficient/harmonious/mindful/clear is communication? Are there processes that can be improved? Where are the hitches? What is the group's time management like?

Depending on what the team's preferences, the reflections of the Team Viewer can be shared directly or moved to a separate meeting.

The Me Viewer/Team Viewer principle can also be applied digitally and communicated before the start of a meeting, either through a chat or agreed-upon symbols. Especially in digital communication contexts, reflection of the meeting structure is often overlooked due to packed agendas. It is important to recognize

---

[3] Breidenbach, Joana/Rollow, Bettina: New Work needs Inner Work, Munich 2019, p. 119.

that communication and attention processes are shaped very differently depending on the medium used.

Especially in times of increased digital communication, hybrid teams, remote work and flexible office hours, it is important for a company, as a team, to keep asking itself: How do we want to use media? Which formats are best suited to each communication medium? How do attention and communication form in the respective medium and how do we deal with it? What do the media we used enabl and what do they hinder in our interactions?

I often observe attempts to translate face-to-face formats into digital platforms without adaption. But *Zoom* is not a lecture hall, *Teams* is not an office, *WhatsApp* is not the break room. Beyond a rhetoric of loss, it is relevant and forward-looking to also ask ourselves at a meta-level: what do media do to our team communication? To our attention? To our creativity? To our presence?

Spaces

Thich Nhat Hanh writes: "Emptiness means to be full of everything, but empty of a separate existence."[1] Before we turn to external, concrete spaces, this quote leads us back inward. Into the inner space, which is always present, available and open. This inner space is explored, discovered, and consciously perceived in meditation, breathing, and mindfulness practices. Breaths and thoughts circulate, sometimes fleeting, sometimes intense, some linger, others pass quickly. Anyone who has meditated knows: The inner space is noisy. One of the biggest misconceptions about meditation is that something is being done "wrong" when the inner voices are loudly heard. Many people think that silence should immediately set in and often too quickly decide, "I can't meditate." However, the purpose of meditation practice is precisely this conscious listening, observing, and perceiving of thoughts and images that fill the inner space.

Directing the gaze inward and closing the eyes to the outside means to hold space for the unheard inner voices, the unseen inner images. The more often this inner space-holding and pausing is practiced, the more peace ensues. The larger the space becomes, the clearer differentiation can be, the more peace is possible within. The emptiness that can then set in over time is never completely empty. It is more like merging with what enables all differentiation and distinction. With the empty side behind thoughts. In which everything is already contained.

"Emptiness means to be full of everything," writes Thich Nhat Hanh. The separate existence, the feeling of separation, dissolves, it is like a sinking and simultaneously rising of consciousness. As one deepens into the inner space, the boundary between inside and outside fades, a feeling of presence arises that completely permeates one's own body and at the same time transcends it. A spaceless experience of space becomes possible.

[1] Thich Nath Hanh: The Art of living, New York 2017, p. 11.

N. Plohr, *Mindful Leadership*, https://doi.org/10.1007/978-3-658-48300-5_15

Words are always merely a makeshift attempt to translate this experience. It does not, without reason, elude differentiation, distinction, and naming through linguistic signs.

I begin this chapter nonetheless with an attempt at description, to sharpen awareness for the inner space. Starting from this, presence sets in, a presence that translates from inside to outside into physical spaces, into communication, into creation. Mindful Leadership practices holding space both inwardly and outwardly.

For example, N. H. told me after our conversation that he regularly meditates. When asked how the practice affects his leadership style, he replied: "Through my meditation practice in the morning, I can better perceive and control my feelings during the day." By holding space for his feelings and moods in the morning and consciously turning to them, he does not carry them uncontrollably into the physical space of the office, but manages, even when he is upset, to deal internally with his emotions, to regulate and classify them.

The space he holds inside, he does not need to take up outside, he does not need an outburst of anger to "vent" his emotions, but takes internal responsibility for his feelings.

With N. H. I was able to talk about spaces on another level, as he himself was significantly involved in the design of his team's office spaces. He places great importance on the employees "not being so boxed in," as he puts it, but being able to move freely. The office floor lets a lot of light into the rooms, all sideboards are a maximum of 140 cm high, there is open seating, small think tanks where groups can come together, the colors are chosen to be natural, many plants complement the picture. "Outer walls can create inner ones," says N. H., emphasizing the importance he places on a feel-good atmosphere. "We have adjustable desks and Bluetooth headphones, so if you have a meeting, you can still walk around and move freely, just lie down on the floor, I've done that too." The "...panoramic view over Hamburg allows openness, you can let your thoughts wander, this allows free thinking and also affects the mindset." There are single chairs in which retreat is possible, "but still signaling: I am still here." He also emphasizes "For me it was important that I don't have to search for my employees. You can retreat, but not hide. It's not about control, but about... openness."

N. H. specifically names the connection between inner and outer space, between open space design, freedom of movement, and free thinking.

What begins with his own practice translates into the office spaces, enabling both retreat and communication. These spaces allow a wide view and at the same time promote concentration.

When I inquired about how working from home affects the team and also his role as a leader, he replied:

"It makes a huge difference. When I'm in the office, employees just stop by or I walk around the area and pick up a lot of things on the side. This virtual distance does make a difference. Many otherwise come to me on the side." The twice-mentioned "on the side" seems at first to be incidental, but it is a point that I have stumbled upon in many conversations about home office. C. P. also says in the interview: “these doorframe conversations that otherwise run on the side… they just fall away!”

Meanwhile, there are increasing attempts to translate these doorframe conversations into digital formats. Additional “informal meetings” are supposed to replace the meeting at the coffee machine or the joint “lunch”. However, the same feeling often does not arise as it does in person, on site. Because even the informal meetings are still tied to the medium of Zoom or Teams or other digital communication tools. Informal and formal gatherings take place via the same channels and even if another digital space is entered and designed, the body is still in the same place, in the same environment, in the same posture. What became particularly clear through the increased digital communication during the pandemic is that some very essential components of communication cannot be transferred to the digital. That other forms of interactions are possible, under different conditions, with different involvements of the body, attention, language, mood and atmosphere.

One of the biggest challenges for hybrid teams, digital meeting culture and remote work structure is to design, use and appropriate these “new spaces” in their own specific way.

For example, the chat function in Zoom can be used to facilitate check-ins and check-outs at the beginning and end of a meeting. The task for the check-in could be to describe one’s emotional state in three words and share them in the chat. *Euphoric. Full of energy. Creative.* Or perhaps: *Hungry. Annoyed. Tired.*

The aim of this brief interaction is not only to “check in” to the meeting, but also to allow the “inner check” and to create space to the question: How am I truly feeling right now? The external framework, the Zoom meeting and the specificity of the chat function make it possible to briefly connect with one’s inner self in this way and articulate one’s emotional state. The medium of Zoom is used in this way to depict a mood snapshot of a group or a team, without delving into deep personal narratives. These can arise after the end of the formal meeting, for instance, when the chat is revisited among team members. “Hey, you mentioned feeling exhausted—should we adress xyz next week?” Such referencing and openness require a fundamental level of trust in each other and are more difficult to establish if team members have not yet met in person.

A reflection for the check-out at the end of a meeting could involve all team members formulating in one sentence what they take away from the meeting. Depending on the group size, this short statement can also be moved to the chat and condensed to the essentials.

The *Virtual Distance,* as N. H. refers to it in the interview, is initially more difficult to overcome, it takes longer until a feeling for the group and one’s own role within it to develop compared to when all participants are physically present in the same room. Check-ins and check-outs are only as helpful as the team chooses to utilize them. They are attempts to enable a multiple perspectives, which often emerge more naturally in physical spaces. M. H., supervisor of N. H. and long-time executive at DB Netze, describes it very precisely in conversation: “You encounter each other in the digital space one-dimensionally and not multi-dimensionally.”

This can also become evident in creative processes. Mihaly Csikszentmihalyi describes how important it is for the experience of flow that feedback loops are continuously generated, in which the environment reacts to the information provided.[2]

Creative flow requires self-assurance, which contributes to a certain order of consciousness and is essential for engaging ini creative productivity. The many small moments of feedback, self-efficacy, reaction on a verbal and also non-verbal level, shift through digital settings, generating new rhythms, delays, but above all uncertainties, which can cause uncertainty and irritation.

Beyond the rhetoric of loss, a first step in reflecting on digital spaces and new forms of exchange is to take a closer look at their specifics and individually decide how they can be used for one's own goals. Breakout rooms, screen sharing, polls, chats and other functions of digital communication not only close off possibilities, but also open up new forms of interaction. Exploring these is an individual process that requires continuous reflection and adjustment.

Questions like these are worth considering:

1. What is the goal of this (digital) meeting?
2. How long can our team maintain concentration in this media setting?
3. How do we use breakout sessions, chats, and other functions?
4. Do we want to use short check-ins and check-outs to express our team's daily form?
5. Is this meeting perhaps more of an email?
6. Conversely, is some email perhaps more of a meeting?
7. What, in our experience, cannot be transferred to the digital realm?
8. Do we need regular offline exchanges and if so: At what rhythm do we meet in physical presence?

To conclude this chapter, I would like to apply the topic of "spaces" very specifically to the reflection of Mindful Leadership practice and divide it into three steps that can be transferred to both offline and online settings.

First: Taking space

In New Work contexts, there is currently a lot of experimentation with keeping hierarchies as flat as possible or even leaving companies to self-organization. What at first sounds like great freedom and also means new freedoms in many respects, on the other hand, also brings new potential for tension. Joana Breidenbach and Bettina Rollo, for example, observe that it can lead to uncertainties if managers do not take their responsibility and *"let power wander diffusely in the team."*[3]

[2] See: Csikszentmihalyi, Mihaly: Flow. The Secret of Happiness, Stuttgart 1992, p. 99 ff.

[3] Breidenbach, Joana/Rollow, Bettina: New Work needs Inner Work, Munich 2019, p. 62.

This diffuse feeling can also occur in digital and analog spaces, for example, when it is not clearly regulated who is leading a meeting or who has which role within a conversation, what the specific goal of the meeting is, etc. To generate and shape a space for exchange, it is helpful and even necessary in many situations to take the existing space and fill it with presence. Being present also means taking space and positioning oneself so that references can be made to each other subsequently.

Practicing presence in one's own inner space also means being able to transfer this presence to outer spaces. Those who regularly consciously turn to the inner, look closely and practice presence, will also be more present in encounters with others and consequently take up more space. This kind of space-taking is different from that of the displayed elbow or the dominating "make-way-attitude". It is a quiet, but clear presence, which is aware of its own presence, ready to take responsibility, but also to give it up. So that power does not wander diffusely, but can be accepted and handed over in a goal-oriented manner, this presence is needed.

Second: Giving space

Once I, as a Mindful Leader, have found my position in the room and assumed power, the question arises as to whom or what space is given. Taking up space is directly linked to the questions: For what purpose? For whom? Which topics do I give space to through my presence? Who is given space within the room, which is also shaped by my presence? I often experience these processes in university contexts when I give seminars, but they can also be observed in group workshops: When I go into a leadership role, accept it, take space, I can subsequently give space and also give up leadership.However, this does not happen "just like that", but only when I make myself visible, am present, and make space shapeable through this presence. Ideally, all team members are aware of their own ability to take and give space. Ideally, an entire team is fully present and in the process capable and willing to both accept and relinquish power, to take and give space. This presupposes that all team members are willing to take responsibility for shaping the space, rather then merely being entertained.

Third: Holding space

This requires a certain maturity that does not shy away from self-reflection, but equally holds *space* inwardly and outwardly. It represents the translation of mindfulness and meditation practice into concrete team processes, meetings, and confrontations, into an environment that may provoke irritations and challenge inner peace. If space is held inwardly for emotions, SIMU's, reactivity, inner storytellers, critics, role patterns, etc., space can be held outwardly for diversity, for differing perspectives, disagreements and contradictions.

The prerequisite for communication at eye level and the recognition of differences is a relaxed and reflective inward gaze that allows internal processes to be recognized and contained, rather than being projected outward uncontrollably. If such an outburst does accure, which is entirely human, it ideally meets a team capable of holding space for it, demonstrating clear boundaries, de-escalating tension, and maintaining stability. Holding space also involves maintaining the balance between inside and outside and taking responsibility for it.

Like all practical models, this three-stage approach is not linearly applicable. It is subject to constant interpersonal negotiation, varying with the day's dynamics, physical space and the team's composition. The aim of this list is to initiate a reflection process, provide a basis for discussion, and raise the question: How do we design spaces in our company?

Belonging

The topic of this chapter became increasingly central through the interviews I conducted for this book. The more detailed my interviewees spoke about leadership, the more often questions came to the fore such as: When do people feel a sense of belonging? As part of a team, a company, an idea? As my interviewee C. P. reported to me: "When people can't contribute, they lack the connection to the company."

Behind this is the basic assumption that people want to contribute and are looking for opportunities to share their ideas and talents. I don't always feel that this trust exists in companies and institutions. Performance thinking is trained early on and grades and test performances are established as evaluation systems. In my university seminars, I often observe that students are so focused on the exams and evaluations that many opportunities for intrinsi motivation or sharing their own ideas pass by.

This is not a reproach to the students, but rather a criticism of our systems, which express belonging and thus implicitly also exclusion through quantified evaluation schemes, instead of inviting participation and co-create. What is evident in the education system often continues in corporate structures. Executives repeatedly tell me that employees are so afraid of not being good enough that they are deprived of the joy of co-creation Can you blame them when for years that very fear was instilled, and at the same time so little space was given for their own ideas? How can this be countered? Promote a rethink and re-action?

What is conveyed by the fear of inadequacy is the need for security. Every team member, including every leadership personality, ultimately has an individual need for security and freedom, which can change depending on the phase of life and age.

Belonging to a company, enterprise, project, idea or team is based, among other things, on the work context allowing the right balance of freedom and security. For example, C. P. describes: "Being able to bring in your own ideas, make your own decisions, act on your own initiative—I had to learn that this is unfortunately not a given. And also how important it is to me."

N. Plohr, *Mindful Leadership*, https://doi.org/10.1007/978-3-658-48300-5_16

For C. P., the need for freedom, for self-design and "self-direction" is so great that she ultimately decides to change her job. Previously, she had attempted several times to create other spaces within the company and to involve the managers in her search process.

When no change is in sight, she draws the appropriate consequences.

"When people can't contribute, they don't feel connected, the turnover is high, everyone goes straight home, the motivation is missing… What should they connect with if they can't contribute with their competencies?"

C. P. knew exactly what she was good at and wanted to do when she was hired. She even communicated what she didn't want to do anymore and why. In the end, she found herself confronted with exactly the tasks she had excluded in the job interview. This led to double frustration, she felt neither heard nor seen: "When you are taken seriously as an employee and your competencies are valued, you naturally feel much more connected to the company and you represent it as if it were your own."

Leadership expert and author Liz Wiseman sums up the feeling that C. P. describes on a meta-level: "people don't wanna be managed, they wanna be led."[1] The difference between management and leadership, according to her definition, lies in how much trust and self-responsibility is given to the employees. If you give them predefined tasks and just let them execute what they are told, team members are *managed*. Leadership, by contrast, creates space employees' own ideas and competencies.

At the same time, teams need a common direction, a vision or overarching task, that allows all competencies to be aligned and integrated. Liz Wiseman succinctly describes the task of leaders in this context as: "giving people context…"[2]. Without context and without a higher-level vision, it is difficult to focus and contribute one's own energies meaningfully. If there is no clear direction, the individual competencies of the team members fray, getting lost in detail, duplicating tasks, or each person pursuing only their own idea. In university project work, I have often experienced that we were given detailed and laborious tasks, but we never knew exactly how these tasks fit into the overall project. We had no "context" and thus no sense of the higher purpose of our actions. Sometimes this direction simply did not (yet) exist, which is not uncommon in research facilities.

But even in these phases of uncertainty and sketching, it is helpful and encouraging to at least get a rough idea of where things can go. This also requires leaders to have the courage to communicate their own uncertainty and to admit when a clear vision is not yet emerging.

Especially in uncertain times, like the ones we are currently experiencing globally, it is not uncommon to have to deviate from certain goals, for visions to rub against unforeseen realities and require reformulation. If this uncertainty is openly

---

[1] Podcast by Brené Brown Dare to Lead: Brené with Liz Wiseman on Impact Players, 18.10.2021, last accessed: 27.06.2022.

[2] Ibid.

communicated, all team members get the opportunity to participate in these orientation phases, to help shape new paths and to work together on solutions.

This openness requires trust and also the willingness to let go of a supposedly all-knowing position as a leader. Rather than feeling the need of having to achieve, know and control everything alone, leaders can help create space for shared exploration, sensing, testing and reorientation.

If there is a strong connection with the company and its vision, this is also reflected in the language, according to C. P.:

"It's always a good sign when we talk about 'we' in the team and also outside the team, even in our free time." The "we" signals of belonging, integrity and shared responsibility. Employees then feel embedded in something larger, as part of a group and not as lone fighters or interchangeable cogs in the corporate machinery.

Questions of belonging always involve reflection on exclusion. Currently, many companies are advocating for more diversity. Social inequality, gender-specific disadvantages and exclusions of people with a migration background must be uncovered and overcome. Especially with regard to the new value orientations of Generation Z, companies need to align with this change in consciousness in order to be seen as an attractive and contemporary employer. The call for diversity is significant, urgently needed and yet also brings new challenges and coping strategies that may not always be effective. The designer and podcaster Maurice Cherry puts it succinctly in a conversation with Debbie Millman: "Diversity and integration are not the same."[3] He reports how he himself was repeatedly and obviously disadvantaged, paid less and fobbed off with menial tasks due to his skin color, even though the agencies he worked for claimed to be open and fair. Company structures are not always overtly discriminatory or disadvantageous. Inequalities often manifest in culture and communication as an unconscious "bias". If, to put it in clichéd terms, only old white men discuss visions, goals and values in the name of diversity, then criticism is appropriate.

Similarly, if, for example, the only woman in the management team prefers to remain silent when it is said that "everyone" could express feedback and criticism, because she knows that her voice is not actually considered equal.

These examples, which stem from concrete observations, are valuable and sometimes uncomfortable questions that every company can ask itself:

- How diverse are "we"?
- Does diversity only exist on paper or does diversity also mean integration for us?
- Whose voices are heard in our company?
- For whom is it difficult to speak freely?
- Where are our blind spots and how do we deal with them?

---

[3]Podcast Debbie Millman: Design Matters: Maurice Cherry, 03.08.2020, last accessed: 27.06.2022.

- How do we manage to increase the diversity of our team and translate it more into everyday company life?
- What does belonging mean to us?

Diversity and belonging in this context encompass not only origin, gender and age, but also to personality structures. M. H., a manager with over twenty years of experience at DB Netze, speaks in an interview with me not only of "employees", but above all of "characters". It is not only important to know whether you have "everyone on board", but also whether "everyone is in the right place". He describes team building processes with the following words: "A team is somehow also a puzzle. And then you know, puzzles where all the pieces are identically, they are for the age group 1-3. So, the more diversity, the more complex and mature the challenge becomes."

The feeling of belonging develops, in his experience, less in the connection with all seventy employees of the company, but through integration into the respective "subproject", which consists of five to six team members. M.H. states, "If a good dynamic is established in these smaller groups, then most of them stay.".

For him as a manager, the central question with new hires is always what the respective team currently needs. He pays attention not only to the resume and professional qualifications, but also to the personal characteristics of the newcomers: "Sometimes I have a certain idea. If I have a team that is very quiet, do I reinforce this quietness or do I bring in someone who stirs things up? Sometimes it's good to get a team moving."

He immediately admits: "If I do that, it can also happen that it gets moving uncontrollably—and of course I have to be able to handle that."

These processes are also a challenge for teams that are constantly reassembling in new and different ways. The increasing turnover rates reflect the new demands that employees place on companies. Work is now much more than just "gainful employment". More and more people seek to "realize" themselves, experience a deeper sense of purpose in their everyday work, and fully develop their individual potentials. This development is certainly progress and a signpost for new forms of work and life. At the same time, the high demands on the workplace can lead to a certain restlessness that counteracts the process of settling in and results in resignation at the slightest dissatisfaction. Belonging takes time and is a process that constantly strives for a new balance and requires the commitment of all involved. Again, it is advantageous if each individual regularly takes the time to pause and ask themselves:

- When do I feel a sense of belonging?
- How much security, how much freedom does my current employment relationship give me and are both needs in balance?
- Do I need a change within my field of duties?
- Is my voice being heard?

- Can I do something to increase diversity and integration in our team?
- How strongly am I connected to the goal and values of the company?
- Do I have enough "context" to carry out my individual task?

To combine both forms of reflection and to get a picture of the mood in the team, an anonymous survey can be helpful, which is then followed up in a face-to-face meeting and summarizes the results for everyone to see. Based on the collected data, it can then be discussed what the team needs to strengthen cohesion and the feeling of belonging. Especially for hybrid teams and digital forms of collaboration, regular exchange about and for the "we-feeling" is reinforcing. C. P. comments on her experiences with home office as follows: "What do you call them? These…door frame conversations are very important—and I keep noticing how much I pick up when I'm on site, really between the lines and you just don't get that in home office."

Belonging, team spirit and a sense of "we-feeling" often develop in subtle moments—between the lines, in door frame conversations, in the corridor, at the coffee machine and in numerous small micro-situations. At the same time, teams need a clear direction, a higher purpose, a context in which they can embed themselves and which provides them with orientation. Micro and macro levels of belonging ideally interlock within the company and fostering both an everyday and overarching feelings of collective progress.

I would like to conclude this chapter with a quote from Brené Brown, who examines the concept of belonging from a deeper perspectivel, linking the inner dimension with the outer. She emphasizes that belonging is a profound sense of trust and self-understanding, which simultaneously recognizing itself as part of a larger whole while also consciously standing alone.

Belonging makes its way from the inside out and begins, as so often, deep within our being: "True belonging is the spiritual practice of believing in and belonging to yourself so deeply that you can share your most authentic self with the world and find sacredness in both being part of something and standing alone in the wilderness. True belonging doesn't require you to change who you are; it requires you to be who you are. "

Recognition

Brené Brown's quote resonates and leads into this chapter. Recognition and belonging are related, as we often seek both at the same time. The affirmation by others, to be exactly right as we are and not otherwise, to be part of something, is a fundamental human longing.

Recognition provides security, self-confidence, and the knowledge: I am seen, I am valuable, I am safe.

At the same time, the topic of recognition, like the topic of belonging, leads into the wilderness, into solitude, and raises questions such as:

- Do I value myself, regardless of the judgment of others?
- What is my relationship with myself like?
- Do I recognize myself?

The Oracle of Delphi already points the way inward: Know thyself, it says, following the traces of ancient mythology. From time immemorial, the task has been to turn towards the inner self, to look closely and to explore and recognize what Brené Brown describes as the "most authentic self".

The recognition of one's own, true self thus begins with the search for this genuine, authentic self, for the individual being-as-it-is, which also recognizes itself independently of external attributions and judgments. It always sounds so simple to "find" that authenticity and to project it outward, to carry it into the world. But what is this real, true self, when are we in contact with it, when do ego needs and other layers overlay our self-perception, and how dependent are we also on external circumstances that each draw a specific picture of authenticity?

Especially in digitalized and quantified practices of certification and confirmation, there is a continuous pull into external perception and performance. This is not only bad, but also provides stages on which the self can explore and experiment, play through affiliations, readjust and find recognition. At the same time, however, these platforms are built on like economies and the judgments of others,

N. Plohr, *Mindful Leadership*, https://doi.org/10.1007/978-3-658-48300-5_17

which can lead to the self-image and also the self-esteem clinging to those judgments. Again, there is a tendency to fall into a codependency that is based on mutual confirmation and loses the reference to the self behind it.[1] If everyone wants and needs to be recognized by everyone in order to feel valuable, authentic relationships are undermined. If, on the other hand, the connection to one's own self is maintained at the same time and recognition is expressed in a way that is willing to *truly* see the other, resonance, connection, and a genuine feeling of affirmation are created.

It is always difficult to argue on a scientific level with the real, authentic, and actual. On the experiential level, however, the difference between recognition that in turn aims at recognition and recognition that truly devotes itself to the other is easier to differentiate. The former form does not involve an energy exchange, often leaving a slightly stale or even exhausted feeling, while the latter facilitates the inward gaze and strengthens self-perception. Genuine recognition allows for an energy exchange and does not deplete resources from either the one who expresses it or the one who receives it.

Genuine recognition for others springs from the inner recognition of one's own self. Following sociological approaches that attribute to today's time the pursuit of external affirmation, such as Dierk Spreen's *Upgrade Culture*[2] or Ulrich Bröckling's concept of the *Entrepreneurial Self*[3], the question arises as to how much awareness and capacity is available to open the gaze for others and to express appreciation.

In several seminars, students recently commented on our discussions on these topics with the following observation: *Somehow, everyone is only concerned with themselves.* This reveals another imbalance that can arise when the gaze is only directed at one's own self, when one works on one's own performance and loses sight of the connection with others. Because beyond codependency, it is a deeply human need to be connected with others, to be seen and to see others.

We will probably never recognize a part of ourselves if we do not also direct our gaze at others, opening and widening ourselves to recognize ourselves in them as well.

What may sound paradoxical is yet another attempt to accommodate the continuous oscillation between inside and outside and to show that recognition, similar to empathy and belonging, knows two directions; inward, towards one's own self, and outward, towards the other as a mirror of shared humanity.

Allowing this very fluctuation and at the same time turning towards the full complexity of one's own inner life brings me back to the practice of mindfulness and insights from yoga philosophy, which intertwine with the theme of recognition. Mindfulness as a practice of presence, of being present, implies a deep recognition of the essence of the present moment. Whill it might sound simple, it is

[1] See also: Sect. 1.8: People Pleasing.

[2] See: Spreen, Dierk: Upgrade Culture. The Body in the Enhancement Society, Bielefeld 2015.

[3] See: Bröckling, Ulrich: The Entrepreneurial Self, Berlin 2007.

often anything but easy to establish amidst the whirl of anticipatory, judging or retrospective thought patterns. This is partly due to the many external stimuli we encounter and partly to the fact that the narrative, evaluative, creative and worrying voice within us is part of our self. This voice is quickly identified as the ego in the Western interpretation and especially in the so-called spiritual scene, from which one should, if one is really serious about mindfulness, try to detach as quickly as possible. This can lead to the ego neither recognized, seen or integrated, but rather suppressed and repelled, often reinforcing ego tendencies behind a spiritual facade. The self-imposed compulsion to free oneself from the ego thus leads directly into an even stronger identification with it.

Yoga philosophy takes a gentler view of the self and its complexity. It assumes two equal parts of the self that need each other and could not exist without each other. One part, Purusha, is the unchangeable part of the self, always relaxed, connected, observing, groundedd and deeply anchored.

The other part, Prakriti, is always changing, seeking, questioning and developing, continually taking on new forms depending on time and environment. Prakriti and Purusha are both equally valuable and important for the human experience and existence. And even though yoga and meditation practices serve the purpose of connecting with the true, highest self, immersing oneself in a space of silence behind all thoughts, the path to this state of consciousness does not bypass Prakriti, but fully recognizes the ever-changing part of the self.

Often yoga beginners ask me after their first meditation experience what they are doing wrong because they can't manage to silence their thoughts—and the answer is: Nothing. This is where mindfulness begins: not in rejecting thoughts, but in allowing them to be, without identifying with them. And this is the tricky part. Because that would mean reducing the self to this part and getting carried away in the jumps and patterns that this part produces. In the balance of Purusha and Prakriti, it is equally recognized that life means change and transformation and that there is a core within it that rests in itself, is deeply rooted and connected.

Recognition at this level also means recognizing both parts of the self equally within oneself. Only through their integration is self-recognition possible.

This also includes all highs and lows, the shadow aspects and also the negatively connoted emotions. Anyone who connects mindfulness practice with walking through life in pure "bliss" misunderstands the concept of presence and acceptance of what is. Whether internally or externally, one of the greatest challenges of presence is to accept and acknowledge it in all its facets.

In the practice of Mindful Leadership, these concepts and philosophical considerations are grounded in practical application. The challenge lies, on the one hand, in perceiving one's own changes becoming aware of how personal development continually impacts one's role as a leader- what feels right and what may no longer fit.

On the other hand, ideally, the holistic persective also extends to team members and employees. In particular, in conversation with M. H., it became clear how important it is to him as a leader to recognize and promote the personal changes and transformations of the employees. This can begin by providing the team with spaces for reflection, allowing them to share their personal development experiences and integrate these into the company's growth. Recognition can also be expressed very concretely in small practices and rituals that go beyond individual feedback conversation and give everyone the opportunity to see and appreciate each other.

How important clear formats are not only for a constructive feedback culture, but also for recognition among each other, became clear to me when I held a workshop with nine executives of a hotel on the topic of communication and self-reflection. At the very end of the day, I asked the group, who had been managing a fully booked hotel over the Easter holidays: What do you need from one other in the coming weeks? Is there something that would support or help you?

After a brief silence, one participant, who had otherwise been very quiet, said: "Recognition." Especially during stressful phases when workloads are high, conversations, that offer encouragement and recognition are often the first to be sacrificedto a tight schedule. Then all energy is focused on one's own responsibilities, the awareness of others narrows and, the overall mood tends to become more irritable. As a result, Rrecognition and appreciation are reduced to afterthoughts, with everyone needing to conserve their own resources.

During the workshop, we developed two techniques together to make it easier for the team to express their appreciation for each other. In regular meetings, the introductory question should no longer be: "What's new, what incidents were there?", but instead: "What went particularly well since the last meeting?"

The two hotel managers emphasized, that recognition, as well as criticism, should not only come from the "top down", but also circulate within, encouraging mutual support, hones feedback and reinforcement., As a playful element in stressful phases, everyone agreed on a "confetti email", which could be sent among each other and sprayed a virtual confetti rain when someone had particularly excelled.

These two techniques are modest examples of how recognition can be integrated into everyday business life. A first step is already taken when teams discuss ways of recognizing one another and acknowledge the importance of the topic. The more spaces for appreciation and recognition of one's own and common developments are created, the easier it becomes be to foster team flow and encourage creativity. An environment of mutual appreciation fosters deep relaxation and trust in one's own self-efficacy—fear cultures and dominant competitive thinking, on the other hand, often lead to mental, physical and creative exhaustion.

Building a culture of recognition and shared appreciation does not mean avoiding criticism or neglecting to set boundaries. On the contrary, thoughtful, constructive criticism is a form of appreciation. It shows genuine engagement with the other person's concerns and projects, seeks the right words and is driven by a well-meaning intention.

At the end of this chapter, I would like to offer two sets of questions that are intended as suggestions for reflecting on one's own self-appreciation and recognition in teams. These questions become lively and practical when they are used as starting points for both personal reflection and collective development.

Recognition of Self

- How well can you accept yourself, just as you are, in this moment just as you are?
- If doubts arise, those "ifs" and "buts" speaks up: What if you didn't need to change anything about yourself, didn't need to achieve anything more, in order to be worthy of your own recognition?
- What if you are just right, exactly as you are?
- Are there successes in your life that you have not sufficiently celebrated and appreciated?
- How about catching up on this?
- What do you appreciate about yourself right now?
- How does your self-appreciation express itself?
- Do you have regular rituals/practices of self-appreciation and self-care?
- Purusha and Prakriti: Which part of you is constant, calm, centered, clear? Which is in motion, seeking change, in transition? Can you connect with both parts of yourself? Accept and recognize yourself as this paradoxical whole?
- In which moments and areas of your life do you wish for more recognition from yourself?
- How can you create space, create a framework, to meet this need?

Recognition in the Team

- Is there a culture of mutual recognition in our team/company/circle of friends?
- How does this culture express itself?
- Are there specific formats/techniques/practices that make it easier for us to share recognition?
- What formats beyond monetary recognition do we use?
- How open are we to recognizing the individuality and diversity of all team members?
- Are there underlying tendencies or dynamics that make appreciation difficult or surpress it?
- Who is given the space to express recognition?
- What do we like to change about our current culture of recognition?

Error Culture

Who doesn't know it? The impulse to stay silent rather thank risk rejection, the fear of making a mistake, that leads us to choose safety over the bold step into the unknown? Holding back unconventional ideas for fear of being laughed at? Not even beginning because the project could fail?

American poet Sarah Kay states: "We need more bad poetry."[1] Not only in the creative industry, but on so many levels, the fear of making a mistake often outweighs the joy of creativeexpression. In the interviews I was conducted for this book, the inevitability of mistakes in professional settings was emphasized again and again. At the same time, many spoke of the fear of failure that permeates teams and management structures alike.

For example, N. H. shared the following with me: "A staff member recently told me that he is always afraid of saying something wrong. And I then told him: But everyone says something wrong sometimes."

I often encounter similar patterns of hesitation in the university context. In seminars, students often begin their responses with a disclaimer: "I don't know if this is what you want to hear, but…" When I explain that most of my questions don't have a singular correct answer and that my intention is to encourage thinking, not testing them, relaxation gradually sets in, more voices speak up and the fears of failure recede. This process usually takes at least half a semester.

What continues to fascinate me is how so called "wrong" answers contribute to a better understanding for everyone each time, once they are accepted, heard and followed without being judged or dismissed. My commitment to create a safe space where no one has to fear sharing a thought also results from many small and large experiences of the opposite. I will never forget how, as a doctoral student, I had worked my way into a completely new theory, connected it to my topic, and shared my thoughts during a colloquium, only to have the entire round of highly

---

[1] Podcast by Debbie Millman Design Matters: Sarah Kay, 17.12.2018, last accessed 27.06.2022.

N. Plohr, *Mindful Leadership*, https://doi.org/10.1007/978-3-658-48300-5_18

titled male participants mock my attempt. I felt powerless, helpless, stupid, and ashamed, which resulted in me turning away from the specific theory and feeling even less encouraged to express my thoughts in future meetings. This did not change even when it was announced at these meetings that it was a "sanction-free space" and "a non-evaluative situation".

My attempt to appreciate the work of the institute where I was getting acquainted and to signal that I was researching for connective capabilities resulted, in my perception, in an experience of humiliation and exclusion. I do not believe that this situation was based on malicious intent, but rather on situational lack of empathy and a group dynamic that served an unconscious *bias* that is reflected in many institutions and companies.

N. H. also refers to educational contexts in his reflections on learned error-avoidance behavior: "In school, you are taught that there is only one correct answer and everything else is wrong. This continues." Again, it probably leads further to research the systemic foundations of this error culture than to condemn teachers and other authorities. In a society based on a quantified rating system in which points are repeatedly awarded for correct answers, in which the red pen circles and supposed misconduct threatens to result in public condemnation, sometimes even defamation, it is only human to want to protect oneself, to share one's own ideas and thoughts only after thorough examination and to erase anything that could potentially be misinterpreted or criticized.

My impression is: There are so many practiced routines and mechanisms that mark the wrong as wrong and on the other hand so few spaces for the sanction-free trying out of what can also be right and important. Perhaps the best ideas, the most appropriate criticism, the finest observations are still wrapped in fearful silence.

So what can be done and especially applied with regard to the design of a Mindful Leadership practice within a business environment?

For N. H., a first step is to show oneself as a leader who is fallible: "To have the courage to say, I have also failed and yes I make mistakes. For me, that's totally part of it. Leadership also means: admitting mistakes."

This reflects the willingness to be brave and to show vulnerability. When leaders reveal that they make mistakes and also how they deal with them, it is much easier for everyone else to be open when doubts, questions or specific misconduct occur.

Towards the end of the conversation, N. H. returns to this aspect. When asked what leaders need to learn before they take on leadership positions, he replies: "Leaders are the ones who will make mistakes, so you also have to be allowed to learn that mistakes are OK."

What sounds so simple here implies a deeper level of understanding and reflection on the kinds of behaviors we learn in response to making mistakes. In many situations, mistakes lead to three extremely unpleasant feelings, often reinforced and mirrored by the environment: shame, guilt, and regret. In the example of the lecture situation, I went through all three. First, the shame of apparently being too stupid to truly understand the theory, I had applied, then a deep feeling of guilt, because it seemed that I alone was responsible for the ridicule I received from others, and finally the regret of having tried to apply the theory at all.

What might now, in retrospect, seem exaggerated and one-sided, felt like the only available response in the described situation. I equated the reactions of others, their lack of empathy, the harsh criticism, and the ridicule of my lecture with contempt for me as a person.

Here is a definition of shame according to Brené Brown: “Shame is the intensely painful feeling or experience of believing that we are flawed and therefore unworthy of love, belonging and connection.”[2]

To counteract shame, according to Brené Brown, requires self- and other-directed empathy, the courage to express feelings of shame, and the mindfulness to avoid over-identification with the emotion. In the situation described earlier, I had no access to these three self-regulation mechanisms. If I could have maintained the connection to myself, it would have been easier to name the inappropriate behavior of others, to be there for myself internally, and to find clear words of demarcation externally. In retrospect, this painful experience is now a basis for being more aware of the complexity of examination situations and also completely different interpersonal encounters.

Thus, the regret I feel in retrospect is no longer tied to the content of my lecture, but to the willingness at the time to let myself be belittled so much.

Brené Brown also has clear words about the feeling of regret: “[…] regret is a fair but tough teacher.”[3] Not regretting anything can mean missingimportant insights that can be derived from the feeling of regret. Not all progress comes in a gentle way and this insight refers not only to individuals, but also to companies and organizations.Making mistakes can be accompanied by regret, guilt, and shame—in an open-minded error culture, it might be impossible to avoid dealing with these feelings. Brené Brown advocates in many ofher books to normalize unpleasant feelings and to develop a language for them. She states:“Shame hates being spoken.”[4] What usually does not help is to forbidthe feeling or to ignore it because it is so unpleasant. Finally, Brené Brown: “Sometimes themost uncomfortable learning is the most powerful.”[5]

Thus, shame, guilt, and regret can bring us valuable insights as part of the holistic experience of being human. However, this requires that painful feelings and the underlying patterns can be openly discussed. This in turn requires mutual trust, self- and other-directed empathy, as well as a good deal of courage.

Closely related to the individual and internal handling of mistakes is the question of how much perfectionism is brought into the activity. An overly high demand on oneself and others brings a correspondingly high sensitivity to errors.

---

[2] Brown, Brené: Atlas of the Heart, New York 2021, p. 137.

[3] Ibid. p. 53.

[4] Ibid. p. 136.

[5] Brown, Brené: Atlas of the Heart, New York 2021, p. 53.

Perfectionism has great advantages when it comes to processing detailed tasks and ensuring quality—but there is a tipping point that leads to the limitation of creative processes and brings chronic dissatisfaction.

If one tends towards perfectionism, it helps to remind oneself again and again that "perfect" looks, tastes, smells, and feels different for every person—and that often enough "perfect" also means choosing the perfectly imperfect.

In perfection, there is a notion of completeness that opposes the flow of creativity and vitality. What is considered perfect today may not be so tomorrow. Perfectionism is the manifestation of what I describe in the chapter "People Pleasing". Perfectionists often pay more attention to others than to themselves or the activity they are currently performing. Healthy striving to do something as well as possible follows an inner impulse and paves the way from the inside to the outside. Perfectionism, on the other hand, is externally oriented and continuously asks the question: What do others probably think of me?

A certain inflexibility with oneself and others is also an indicator of perfectionism. A healthy striving for the best result still allows for joy and serenity, perfectionism often results in physical and mental tension.

Here again, a mindfulness exercise can be applied, specifically the principle of *non-attachment*,. What is meant by this is that one's own feelings and thoughts are perceived, but not clung to or overly identified with. The simple yet far-reaching realization behind this is: You are not your thoughts and you are not your feelings. You are not your shame, not your guilt, not your regret. Nor are you your perfectionism. You are the silence behind all feelings and thoughts. Meditation and mindfulness practice is the recurring reminder of this awareness.

In cultivating non-attachement, over-identifications with mistakes can relax, because a space emerges that allows all arising feelings and thoughts and at the same time does not confuse them with one's own identity. In a trusting and reflective environment, it is possible to remind each other of this perspective, to openly discuss perceived mistakes, and to jointly search for solutions.

Mindful Leadership starts exactly here as a practice and holds both the space for individual inner development and for conscious handling of mistakes at the team level.

I would also like to conclude this chapter with several blocks of questions and a small inspiration for an internal team format.

Individual Error Culture

1. How do you deal with mistakes when you make them?
2. What feelings and reactions arise in you?
3. Can you forgive yourself easily?
4. What helps you with the process of forgiving?
5. What patterns in dealing with mistakes do you know by yourself?
6. Are there mistakes that you have ignored and suppressed in the past?
7. What can you still learn from them now?

Error Culture in Teams

1. Are there formats in which you talk about mistakes?
2. Are you open to learning from mistakes?
3. What are the biggest insights you have already derived from mistakes?
4. How do you behave towards each other when mistakes happen?

"Safe Spaces"

1. How safe do you feel in your team?
2. How open and vulnerable can you show yourselves?
3. Is it possible to openly admit mistakes?
4. Are the "safe spaces" equally safe for all members?
5. Who can afford to make mistakes, who perhaps cannot?
6. How can the gradient be adjusted if necessary?

Fool's Freedom

Meet in a familiar environment where you feel comfortable. Agree that for the time of your gathering, there will be no evaluation, judgment, or criticism, but only sharing. Tell each other all the uncommon ideas that are languishing in the inner desk drawer because they seemed too crazy to voice. Allow yourselves fool's freedom.

Meet again after a set period of time and discuss what inspired you about the supposed craziness, which idea has stayed in your memory, and whether something can be made from one or another approach.

In conclusion, a thought that reminds us of the entire range of human emotions and experiences. Every emotion needs a counterpoint to be experienced in its specificity. What would joy be, if there was no sadness? What would serenity be, if anger was not known? What would love be, if we never experienced fear? And what would, to return to the topic of this chapter, success and joyful accomplishment be, if experiences with mistakes were absent?

Courage

In response to the question of what qualities leaders need, I received the same answer over and over again: courage.

M. H. directly links the relevance of courage to the willingness to make mistakes: "We have very narrow guardrails in the company. You can cling to the handrail all the time, but I want my people to jump sometimes. I always say I am the evacuation team and will get you out. Every leader, but also every working student needs courage. Courage to make mistakes."

The self-designation as an evacuation team shows that M. H. considers it part of his task to trust employees and team leaders to make decisions on their own and to take responsibility even in uncertain moments. In our conversation, he shares the observation that the willingness to be courageous is giving way to an increasing need for security. He attributes this change partly to the internal development of the company and its value orientation, but also places it in a larger context that takes into account the coronavirus pandemic and a basic need for security in uncertain times. The introductory quote from our conversation shows that M. H. views courage as something that can be practiced, indeed must be practiced, when one cannot feel safe and when it is not foreseeable how the future will develop.

In my research on the topic of courage, it became increasingly clear that courage can manifest in very different facets and extends far beyond classic hero stories and epic bravery. Courage can show itself in very small situations and moments, courage is often not recognizable as courage at first glance, courage is often quiet and has little to do with tests of courage and recklessness. Courage is as individual as it is diverse. What appears courageous to one person may not be so for another. Is it courageous when an adventurer jumps off a bridge? Is it courageous to take an unnecessary risk? Is it courageous when extroverted personalities give speeches and comfortably present themselves on a stage?

N. H. told me in our conversation that he was very shy in his school days, always holding back for fear of saying something wrong.

N. Plohr, *Mindful Leadership*, https://doi.org/10.1007/978-3-658-48300-5_19

He is now in a leadership position, shares responsibility for eighty employees, often speaks in front of groups, conducts individual conversations, and actively approaches others when he feels that someone might need to talk.

"The strength I took from my shyness is, I withdraw and observe." The retreat, which used to serve him as a shield, is now an observation tool in his current position. The experience with his own shyness allows N. H. to develop a high degree of empathy for employees who are struggling with similar feelings and who practice silence for fear of making mistakes. What this process reveals is a fundamental intertwining of courage and vulnerability, which Brené Brown sums up as follows: "You can't get to courage without rumbling with vulnerability."[1]

In this quote, the "rumbling" is of crucial importance. In Brené Brown's usage, "to rumble" means to grapple with one's own vulnerability, to step into the feeling of vulnerability, not to overly identify with it, but to deeply understand it, to uncover one's own patterns and to learn from them. Courage, in turn, is linked to the willingness to grapple with one's own vulnerability. Since vulnerability shows itself as diverse and individual, it is virtually impossible to decide in advance which actions are courageous and which are not. Courage needs context.

The example of N. H. makes clear how his confrontation with his own shyness could transform into a strength that now enables him to encourage others when they come to him with similar experiences. Vulnerability does not mean getting caught up in one's own emotional world and overly identifying with it. In the case of N. H., this would mean that every time an employee reveals her shyness, he himself would fall back into the feeling or share all the moments when he himself was shy. Being vulnerable does not mean revealing everything unfiltered for the sake of vulnerability. This form of emotional outburst has nothing to do with courage, but rather with a lack of reflection on one's own boundaries and those of the listeners. Brené Brown also has clear words for this: "Vulnerability minus boundaries is not vulnerability, It's confession, manipulation, desperation, or shock and awe, but it's not vulnerability."[2]

If courage and vulnerability are so closely related, then a significant part of being courageous lies in dealing with one's own vulnerability, which in turn makes it possible to share one's own experiences with others or to embody them silently without dumping them on the environment. Courage, in the best case, also encourages others and does not rob them of energy or manipulate them on the basis of one's own emotional outburst.

In the process of "rumbling" as an internal confrontation with vulnerability, mindfulness as quiet inner turning and listening is helpful again. Because it requires a certain distance, a being-aware and being-present with what is going on inside. This reflection without evasion, the clear, present looking and taking responsibility is courageous.

---

[1] Brown, Brenè: Dare to lead, London 2018, p. 2.

[2] Brown, Brenè: Dare to lead, London 2018, p. 39.

Courage is often associated with strength. Tracing courage in leadership contexts, the question arises: What is strength? Who is perceived as a strong leadership personality? And how has this perception changed over time? What kind of strength do we need nowadays?

Brené Brown describes how over time an image of leadership work has developed that resembles armor. Out of fear of injury and loss of face, out of fear of not having all the answers to all questions, out of fear of not knowing where to go, leaders (and not only leaders) put on an armor of old beliefs, perfectionism, cynicism, and arrogance, which results in a practice that Brown calls *armored leadership* and marks the opposite of productive, courageous vulnerability, *daring leadership*.[3]

We all learn protective mechanisms throughout our lives that contribute to strengthening our shield, many of them we unconsciously incorporate into our armor and eventually wonder why we can hardly move for all the protection. A heavy armor robs thinking, feeling, and acting of flexibility. It protects against potential enemies, but also avoids real closeness, touch, and openness. An emotional armor, which may have proven useful in some situations, can quickly become a high wall, behind which the heart and mind are protected, yet unreachable and ultimately lonely. Leadership strength does not hide behind thick walls, but shows itself openly, humanly, vulnerably, and responsibly. Courage in this context also means being able to set clear boundaries without lowering the visor and going into battle.

Courage, like vulnerability, initially has little to do with winning or losing. Rather, it shows the willingness to do something without knowing whether it will succeed. Simon Sinek writes: "The courage to lead is the willingness to take risks for the good of an unknown future."[4]

Even if some times feel more uncertain than others: We can never really *know* what the future holds. In this respect, every moment, every instant is an opportunity to practice being courageous. What may sound banal knocks on the door of deep, very human fears of loss of control, change, and ultimately always: death and transience. We want to lull ourselves into safety and yet we know we can't. So part of *armoured leadership* is also wanting to hold on to the "old and proven" at all costs and vehemently resisting changes of all kinds. Courage, on the other hand, means accepting the fundamental impermanence of life and even finding joy in it.

Thich Nath Hanh writes: "Impermanence is something wonderful. If things were not impermanent, life would not be possible. A seed could never become a plant of corn; the child couldn't grow into a young adult; there could never be healing and transformation; we could never realize our dreams. So impermanence is very important for life. Thanks to impermanence, everything is possible."[5]

---

[3] See: Brown, Brenè: Dare to lead, London 2018, p. 76 f.

[4] Sinek, Simon: The Infinite Game, USA 2019, p. 199.

[5] Thich Nath Hanh: The Art of living, London 2017, p. 116.

In leadership contexts, there is often talk of the so-called *fixed* or *growth Mindset*. While the former sticks to known strategies and tries to respond to new challenges with old methods, the growth-oriented mindset is open to creative reactions and solutions. Behind this lies first and foremost the deep acceptance of the unpredictability of circumstances. A deep acceptance of what is. In the sense of Thich Nath Hanh, all living things have a fundamental impermanence. He goes beyond the acceptance of change and describes it as *wonderful*. The wonders of life, creation, development are deeply connected with *impermanence*.

Interestingly, positive psychology assigns the subcategory of enthusiasm to courage.[6] Being able to meet the world with enthusiasm and energy is an expression of courage. This ability to be enthusiastic can also be read in the lines of Thich Nath Hanh, because he does not turn away from change in fear, but welcomes it and appreciates it as the breeding ground for all living things.

Courageous leadership work, courageous collaboration, courageous action, thinking and doing does not start with loud, offensive heroic deeds, but with a quiet acceptance and joy in the face of change.

Other subcategories that belong to courage in the sense of Positive Psychology are: Authenticity as courage for truth, bravery as the courage to face challenges, and perseverance, as the courage to commit to a project and bring it to completion.[7]

To conclude and transition to the practical part of this chapter, I would like to return to the quote from M. H. mentioned at the beginning: "Courage… I believe is something we will need to practice in the near future."

This raises the question: Can courage be practiced? And if so, how? The mentioned subcategories of courage provide some clues and can be reformulated into the following reflection questions:

Instead of a test of courage…

- How authentically do we communicate in our team?
- How well can we face challenges?
- Do we bring our projects to completion? How good is our perseverance?
- How enthusiastically do we look towards the future?
- How well can we cope with change?
- Is instability something that brings us joy or rather triggers fear?

These questions implicitly contain the ability to be courageous and each opens a context in which courage can be demonstrated and practiced.

To further explore the topic of courage and reflect on it within the team, I recommend taking a moment to collectively answer the question: What is courage?

[6] Personality Psychology and Diagnostics, University of Zurich: https://www.charakterstaerken.org/VIA_Interpretationshilfe.pdf, last accessed: 27.06.2022.

[7] Ibid.

Write down, each for themselves: Courage is…

Then collect all the notes, mix them up, and pin them to a wall so you can look at them together. Look for intersections that can be summarized into characteristics and clusters.

Afterwards, ask yourselves the questions: How can we integrate courage even more into our daily business routine? Where are we already courageous? Do we handle courageous decisions responsibly? What do we need to be more courageous?

Trust

Perhaps the chapter heading is already a possible answer to the last question asked. Not without reason, the German word for trust also implies the verb *to dare.* When trust is given, one dares to be open, to show oneself, to share one's thoughts and feelings. Trust requires courage, and courage requires trust.

In Brené Brown's work, vulnerability, courage, and trust are closely intertwined. She describes a similar interplay of mutual reinforcement between trust and vulnerability.

"We need to trust to be vulnerable, and we need to be vulnerable to build trust."[1] Those who trust dare to open up and make themselves vulnerable. In work contexts, trust often goes "ahead of the game" and follows an intuitive feeling before the person who is given the trust gets the opportunity to confirm it. I have often experienced that superiors gave me their trust when hiring me and communicated this openly. My feeling, in turn, formed as a reaction to the given trust as increased responsibility for my tasks.

Leaders are constantly involved in building and giving trust. Trust forms continuously, it grows over time and always requires mutual confirmation.

Brené Brown summarizes her findings on the subject of trust as follows: "[…] I had always assumed that trust is earned in big moments and through really grand gestures, not the more simple things […] It turns out that trust is in fact earned in the smallest moments. It is earned not through heroic deeds, or even highly visible actions, but through paying attention, listening, and genuine care and connection."[2]

To earn and build trust, it is not enough to prove oneself as trustworthy once. We all need the recurring attention for each other, the empathy for the other person, the listening and staying connected, to sustainably promote trust.

---

[1] Brown, Brenè: Dare to lead, London 2018, p. 30.

[2] Brown, Brenè: Dare to lead, London 2018, p. 32.

N. Plohr, *Mindful Leadership*, https://doi.org/10.1007/978-3-658-48300-5_20

The psychologist and relationship analysis expert John Gottmann describes those very small moments and opportunities to work on mutual trust as *Sliding door moments*. These moments can be summarized as micrological decision-making processes between "turning away or being there."[3] We all know these situations where the opportunity arises to be there for employees, friends, partners, fellow human beings. Sometimes we have no capacities and protect our own boundaries by turning away. However, if we keep turning away again and again, the relationship is gradually deprived of its nourishment.

On the other hand, trust is built when we turn to the person and signal to them again and again that we are there, listening, taking them seriously, and making a connection. These *Sliding door moments* are harder to perceive when teams meet exclusively in digital contexts. Body language, small gestures, the complete facial expression—all this contributes to following the intuitive decision and maintaining openness for each other.

N. H. tells me in our conversation how often he "just walks across the floor and sees if someone is bothered by something." He actively approaches his employees, offers his presence and a conversation when he feels it could be helpful. He took over his position in the home office and immediately asked himself how he could gain the trust of his remote working team members. In the conversation, he shares and explains the strategy he developed: "The question I asked myself was: I have 50 people sitting in the home office, how do I gain their trust? And also, what is trust actually? And clearly, trust is created when you signal, I am there for you, but actually classically according to the iceberg model, trust is created when we go below the water surface. And I knew, if I want their trust, I have to open up, go below my water surface. Only if I make myself vulnerable, can I be authentic, can I be a good leader. And what I did, I wrote to everyone: Ask me the most uncomfortable question you can think of. And then I took an hour for each one, all fifty, and called them, because I wanted us to get into a conversation on a personal level."

N. H. gives an advance in openness and vulnerability to gain the trust of his team. The invitation to ask an uncomfortable question opens a space for the employees to start a conversation and get to know N. H. better. It is more of a *big moment,* a constructed moment for building trust, which responds to a specific situation (the home office and the digital communication situation). What N. H. communicates with this step is the willingness to open up, to be approachable and accessible. But above all, it does not stop with the one big trust-building gesture.

N. H. shows himself, as soon as the COVID-19 regulations allow it, also in the presence situation approachable and open, actively approaches his team members and continues his reflection on trust. He describes how the first conversation based on the uncomfortable question opened the door, and how his presence in the company's everyday life kept it open.

[3] Ibid. p. 33.

At least one fundamental characteristic of a Mindful Leader flows into N. H.'s approach: The ability and willingness for self-reflection and reflection on the question: What is trust? Mindful Leadership requires the courage and also the self-confidence to turn inward, to deal with one's own issues *below the water surface*. The clearer the inward gaze is and remains, the more space can also be held for the concerns and emotions of employees.

If one applies John Gottmann's definition of trust to self-trust, *sliding door moments* can also be identified in the relationship with oneself and one's own needs. Moments when we can either be there for ourselves or turn away, strengthen or undermine the connection to ourselves. Every day offers countless opportunities in which we can develop responsibility, intuition, and sensitivity for our needs and emotions. And as in any other relationship, we depend on giving ourselves the experience over and over again that we can rely on ourselves, listen to ourselves, and be there for ourselves.

This is anything but egocentric. On the contrary, it is the prerequisite for being there for others and building trust. How could we trust someone who denies trust to themselves?

Here too, mindfulness practice plays a crucial role, because only with the conscious perception and acceptance of what is, can the relationship with oneself be strengthened and trust can develop. So it starts once again with active listening, and perceiving. Inward and outward.

At the team level, mutual trust not only has positive effects on social interaction, but also on performance, creativity, and the desire for innovation.[4] Trust enables admitting mistakes, learning from them, sharing ideas, making bold suggestions, and sharing constructiv critique. Simon Sinek writes: "When leaders are willing to prioritize trust over performance, performance almost always follows. However, when leaders have laser-focus on performance above all else, the culture inevitably suffers."[5]

A leadership style based on fear and pressure, demanding too much from employees and only aiming at performance, will never establish a culture that sustainably promotes trust and creativity. Mindful Leadership, on the other hand, enables and embodies the courage to trust oneself and others, to learn from mistakes, and to show vulnerability without loosing an awareness for boundaries.

A corporate culture based on trust requires a clear value orientation, a sensibility for *sliding door moments*, and leaders who are willing to share their power, delegate responsibility, and sometimes hold back.

M. H. says in conversation with me: "As a leader, I must be able to let go. And also endure it and let them run. Rules clear… But it also needs people who say OK, I know the processes, but I'm going this way now."

The self-confidence to seek and follow one's own paths is supported by an environment in which trust is given and cultivated. In *Trusting Teams,* as Simon

---

[4] Cf.: Sinek, Simon: The infinite game, USA 2019, p. 107.

[5] Ibid. p. 130.

Sinek calls them, all team members take responsibility for a culture of trust—in small as well as large moments of interaction.

Self-confidence is closely linked to self-care, with mindfulness for one's own needs, potentials, and limits. From the conscious handling of one's own resources, self-efficacy emerges and thus closes the circle to the first part of this book. From increased self-efficacy, a solid self-confidence grows, which can also be transferred to other team members.

Trust requires continuity. Due to the coronavirus pandemic and its multifaceted consequences, many companies are losing their familiar structure or it is in the process of changing. It is all the more important to cultivate and strengthen basic values and characteristics that can be continuously developed despite all external changes.

The following trust questions are therefore intended to be asked again and again, to be answered anew, and perhaps to stimulate new reflections and conversations based on their answers.

Reflection questions

1. How well can you rely on yourself?
2. What strengthens your self-confidence?
3. How reliable are you for others?
4. Sliding door moments: Are you there for yourself or do you turn away?
5. Are there recurring typical sliding door moments at work?
6. How do these occur and what is your reaction?
7. Write on small notes in the team:
8. What are sliding door moments for you in everyday business life?
9. On a scale of 1–10, how high would you rate the mutual trust in the team?

Collect the results covertly and then make them visible on a pinboard for everyone. Start a conversation about what trust means to you and how it is practically expressed and maintained in everyday life.

Share the results with new employees as well to introduce them to your value system and your corporate culture.

Trust forms the roots of interpersonal relationships. Once these are torn out, they rarely come back. If they are, however, widely branched and deeply anchored, nature can unfold its full growth. Trust needs mindfulness, care, attention, and continuity. The process of building trust is never finished, it is maintained through loving attention.

Sustainability

Mindfulness practices are now strongly associated with a highly individualized practice. At first glance, mindfulness seems to be part of the diverse trends towards personal development, energy management, and self-optimization. However, at its core, it contains a fundamental quality that goes far beyond self-centeredness.

As I pointed out in the first part of the book, Thich Nath Hanh's concept of *Interbeing* is crucial. Mindfulness leads us into the present moment, towards what is, what surrounds us, and what we can sensually perceive and experience. Mindfulness as a practice is the art of being present and connecting with the vitality available in every moment. This includes a dimension that goes beyond the self, beyond the ego, and beyond turning towards it. Experiencing vitality and being present also means becoming aware of the interplay and coexistence. The *Interbeing* with other beings, our environment, even things and objects, is reflected in a mindful interaction with everything to which we feel connected.

Conversely, if we feel unconnected, it is very unlikely that we will interact respectfully, mindfully, and consciously with our environment. The introductory quote from Thich Nath Hanh suggests that we tend to become less mindful over time of the beauty that surrounds us daily. This can be seen in long-standing relationships with partners, or as Thich Nath Hanh describes it, in our relationship with nature: "We are so close to earth, that sometimes we forget how beautiful it is."[1] We are so close to it that we no longer appreciate its beauty and resources and tend to take them for granted. Instead of deepening our relationship with nature and respecting it, honoring its regenerative cycle (of which we are part), we are still too busy translating it into contested ownership and exploiting it for the prosperity of individuals. Thich Nath Hanh recognizes a deep, twisted longing for freedom behind the fights against nature, against other nations, and ultimately against ourselves: "The freedom we seek is not the kind of freedom that is self-destructive

[1] Thich Nath Hanh: The art of living, London 2017, p. 6.

N. Plohr, *Mindful Leadership*, https://doi.org/10.1007/978-3-658-48300-5_21

or destructive of other nations or environments, but the kind of freedom that liberates us from loneliness, anger, hatred, fear, craving, and despair."[2]

A feeling of deep connection cannot be replaced by any possession. This realization is confirmed to me again and again in my coaching sessions when people who are materially rich still feel inwardly empty, unfree, and not truly happy. Of course, this does not mean that the pursuit of material success is fundamentally wrong or cannot also be associated with deep happiness.

In the sense of *Interbeing*, the question arises in connection with worldly wealth: What does the wealth of individuals contribute to the well-being of all? And how is the money, the success generated? Are human or natural resources exploited to acquire one's possessions? Or is a contribution made that is valuable for everyone while also generating economic profits?

There is nothing wrong with the frequently and briefly formulated corporate goal: growth. At the same time, however, the question arises: growth of what, for what, and with what? The entire field of post-growth economics deals with these questions and invites us to redefine growth or at least question the previous coupling of the term to a monetary goal. Niko Paech mentions in his "Principles of a Post-Growth Economy" as the first point: decluttering and deceleration. He asks the question in short: From which goods and productions can our system free itself?[3] What do we really need and above all how much of it? And is the continuous acceleration of production and communication processes always synonymous with success, progress, and efficiency?

These questions can not only be asked at a higher systemic or societal level but ultimately in every organization, every institution, every company—and also in everyday personal life. From post-growth economics, the concept of resonance according to Hartmut Rosa emerges, which I have already mentioned in the first part of this book. Resonance describes the deepening relationship with the things and people that already surround us.[4] Instead of accumulating more to possess more, resonance enables the vibrating, lively relationship with everything that is already there.

Resonance and mindfulness are related in this acceptance and appreciation. Also the moment of deceleration is included in both. Likewise, the relating to other people, but also to nature and objects. Going beyond oneself thus becomes a tangible essential part of self-formation. While Hartmut Rosa writes of a sociology of world relations, Thich Nath Hanh sharpens awareness for our interbeing.

Sustainability in our consumer-oriented world is far more than a trend. It is a necessity to make individual and entrepreneurial decisions that follow a resource-oriented consciousness. This begins, as so often, with respecting one's own, very

---

[2] Thich Nath Hanh: The Art of living, London 2017, p. 6.

[3] Paech, Niko: Principles of a Post-Growth Economy (2009), http://www.postwachstumsoekonomie.de/material/grundzuege/, last accessed: 27.06.2022.

[4] See: Rosa, Hartmut: Resonance. A Sociology of World Relation, Berlin 2016. p. 281 ff.

human energy reservoirs. For example, when I think about politicians coming together completely drained, overtired and exhausted at night to vote on the future of natural resources, I wonder: How can a system be changed at the top of which self-exploitation is the rule?

Kevin Kühnert says in an interview: "[…] we only hold up a mirror to society."[5] But isn't it the other way around? Isn't it a twisted image of leadership that equates certain positions with the willingness to sacrifice and blur the boundaries of work? Doesn't "society" also follow the leaders it produces? Where does change begin then? Can we equally appreciate our own resources, those of our fellow human beings and those of the environment? And if we don't start soon, when will we?

In us as individuals, who have always lived in co-existence with each other, there is also a level of interbeing. Thich Nath Hanh writes: "[…] you cannot take the mind out of the body, and you cannot take the body out of the mind. They inter-are."[6] If one considers the complexity of the human body, its neuronal, muscular and organic structures and all that which in German can only be translated somewhat awkwardly as "mind", then we are already living interbeings within ourselves. Bringing the various elements of our individual being into harmony resembles the overarching task of conscious interaction with each other. Mindfulness practices are about experiencing body and mind as a whole and holding space for inner diversity. Who doesn't know that mental patterns affect the physical state and vice versa?

In this context, sustainability also means respecting one's own rhythms, strengthening physical and mental resources and acknowledging one's own (stress) limits. In teams and organizations, the corresponding task is to know and appreciate internal group dynamics.

Individuals and companies rarely follow a linear logic of increase in their development, but rather cyclical phases.

Similar to a spiral, projects and personal life stages repeatedly go through stages of alignment, implementation, evaluation and reflection, each of which takes different forms.

These cycles always include breaks, moments of pausing, reflecting and starting anew. Looking at the growth processes of nature, it becomes obvious that retreat, the time of slowing down, of re-sowing and rooting, is just as important as the spring-like sprouting and blooming. Nature does not grow linearly, but cyclically. How could we do it differently?

These metaphorical considerations tie in with another criticism of the post-growth economy, which, in addition to the concept of growth, also subjects that of progress to closer scrutiny. For a long time, progress was equated with (technological) acceleration, but we have now reached a point where the following question

---

[5] Podcast: Hotel Matze: Kevin Kühnert: Do you believe everything you say, 06.04.2022, last accessed: 27.06.2022.

[6] Thich Nath Hanh: The art of living, London 2017, p. 24.

is justified: Acceleration towards what? Acceleration from what? And somewhat more broadly: What is progress?

Media scientist Paul Virilio already painted a bleak picture in 1990 of the *racing standstill,* in which any accelerating logic of increase threatens to get out of control and be elevated to an end in itself.[7] The question is, how much acceleration is useful and can maintain a balance of human and ecological resources?

Somewhat more gently, but no less remarkably, the protagonist Kao-tai in the novel *Letters into the Chinese Past* shares his observations: "They cannot be dissuaded from the idea that the new is always inevitably better than the old. Progress… They progress, they progress. From everything. They progress from themselves? Why? I wonder. Probably only because they don't like being with themselves."[8] What the novel character expresses can be transformed beyond fiction into the very concrete question: Where are we progressing to?

Growth and progress are two principles that shape our (industrial and technological) culture, continuing down to the individual level. There is nothing wrong with wanting to develop and grow. And yet: For what? Where to? At what cost?

Growth and progress require a fundamental awareness of the interconnectedness of our world. Media scholar Marshall Mc Luhan already spoke of the *global village*[9], the idea that digital technologies in particular can contribute to a change in consciousness continues, among others, with Michel Serres[10].

The emerging utopia, the hope for a progressive thinking that also commits to interbeing, is also reflected in the words of Thich Nath Hanh: "We have the power to decide the destiny of our planet […] It is our insights and our actions that will save us. If we awaken to our true situation, there will be collective change in our consciousness. Then hope will be possible."[11]

A collective change process often begins on a small, everyday scale. One way for companies to approach the topic of sustainability is to start with very basic questions about how to handle their own internal resources. It is helpful if each team member first records a few reflections for themselves, and then enters into an exchange.

Here are a few suggestions

- How well can you manage your energy?
- Do you have a sense of when you need a break?

---

[7] Virilio, Paul: Racing Standstill, Berlin 2008.

[8] Rosendorfer, Herbert: Letters into the Chinese Past, Munich 1986, p. 93.

[9] McLuhan, Marshall, Powers, Bruce R.: The Global Village. Transformation in World Life and Media in the 21st Century, Oxford 1989.

[10] Serres, Michel: Invent yourself anew! A declaration of love to the networked generation, Berlin 2013.

[11] Thich Nath Hanh, The Art of living, London 2017, p. 24.

- Do you take enough breaks?
- How well do you know your rhythm? When are your typical peak times during the day, when can you be most creative and when do you need rest?
- Can you enbody your natural rhythm?
- What do you need to recharge your energy?

Switching from the individual level to the team level, I would like to mention and explain three stages of collaboration derived from developmental psychology. They go beyond internal corporate structures and can be applied to any interpersonal relationship. Moreover, they can provide suggestions for dealing with the relationship with oneself and life.

1. Competition:
   Following the principle of displacement, people and organizations confront each other in a competitive manner at this stage. Encounters serve as a battleground for power and strength. This can also be expressed within the team, for example, when a ranking of specific performances is carried out, positions and power are fought for, and a strong hierarchical thinking is promoted. The energy of others is generally perceived as a threat. Even on a personal level, this competitive thinking can come to the fore, for example, when competing with a previous performance or if the curriculum vitae follows a one-upmanship mode.
2. Cooperation:
   There is cooperation with the other team members, an agreement on peaceful coexistence is reached, and initial steps towards collaboration are possible. However, the perspective still tends to stick to one's own ideas and objectives, the prevailing question is: How does cooperation serve me/us? The energy of others is recognized as a possible additional resource and, if possible, put into one's own service.
   On a personal level, cooperation is an acceptance of one's own life course, a more relaxed retrospection is possible, and even difficult phases are dealt with.
3. Co-creation:
   Collaboration becomes co-creativity. One's own energy and individuality are experienced and used in connection with others. Differences and diversity are seen as the breeding ground for creative processes. It is possible to implement ideas alone as well as to contribute and bring in individual resources for a higher goal. Within the team, good energy management is maintained, the team rhythm is observed and taken into account in annual planning. Often there are industry-specific stress phases—how do you as a team deal with these? What are typical stress patterns of your team? How can you prevent and counteract them in advance?
   At the level of co-creation, the least energy is used for unnecessary power struggles. Resources are used in such a way that they serve the common goal, and decision-making processes and leadership work circulate depending on

competence and project situation. This stage requires a high degree of personal responsibility, self-reflection, and trust from all participants. Beyond the internal co-creations, the question can be added: How well do we co-create with natural resources? With the needs and necessities of our time? With other companies that pursue a similar goal as we do?

Decisions

To directly connect to the previous chapter: The stage of co-creation does not automatically imply that decisions are always made by consensus or that all team members are equally involved in every decision-making process at all times. However, it does prompt a new level of reflection on how decisions are made.

Joana Breidenbach and Bettina Rollow write: "Making decisions by consensus is inappropriate in many situations. Not only do they take too long, but they often result in the lowest common denominator."[1] Instead, the authors propose a more contemporary approach: to acknowledge the experiences already present in the team and integrate them into decision-making processes. This relieves managers and removes the pressure to make every complex decision from the top.[2]

To effectively transfer decision-making power, it must first be consciously accepted and actively assumed. Power that floats around aimlessly causes more confusion and insecurity than the freedom to make decisions. Therefore, restructuring decision-making processes requires a clearly defined framework.

Joana Breidenbach and Bettina Rollow name three formats for the distribution of decision-making power[3].

1. Role-based decisions:
   Depending on the "role" or position, certain decision-making powers are granted. If this company-oriented view of job descriptions is supplemented with sociological role theory, each role comes with certain freedoms, but also challenges. These are subject to continuous change within the system and require constant re-examination. For example, how have the internal roles within the company changed under remote work circumstances? How does this change also affect decision-making processes?

[1] Breidenbach, Joana/Rollow, Bettina: New Work needs Inner Work, Munich 2019, p. 54.

[2] Ibid.

[3] Ibid. p. 113 f.

N. Plohr, *Mindful Leadership*, https://doi.org/10.1007/978-3-658-48300-5_22

2. Consensus-oriented decisions:
   All team members are equally involved in the decision. In votes, it can be quantified in which direction the decision-making process is heading. For more complex questions, an anonymous survey can be helpful, in which all team members give a brief written statement. All statements are collected and coded together, sorted by preferences and topics, and then translated into a concrete decision.
3. Competence-based decisions:
   In this process, team members have different amounts of voting share and decision-making power depending on their competence. There is a commitment to seek the advice of other employees when they have more knowledge, experience, or expertise.

All three forms can be part of co-creative team structures. However, the more freedom there is to switch between formats, the more personal responsibility is taken within teams and the less competition prevails. In particular, the third format requires recognition of the expertise of other team members and the admission of one's own competence limits.

In the context of a Mindful Leadership practice, the question arises which format responds best to the given situation. Mindfulness as a turning towards the present moment, towards what is, makes it possible to ask and continually question whether the chosen structure still meets the current challenges.

In addition, mindfulness can help to slow down the decision-making process. Often wrong decisions are made because they bow to the (perceived or very concrete) time pressure. This can then possibly lead to strenuous and time-consuming repair measures in the long term or to a revision of decisions, which in turn can undermine trust in decision-making competence.

To prevent these loops and irritations, it can be helpful to use a tool that Brené Brown suggests for improving decision-making: The simple yet efficient **Time-Out.**[4] In her organization, all members have the opportunity to pull the Time-Out card and call for distance in difficult discussions and decision-making processes and to meet again afterwards. Especially in group dynamics, it can happen that the internal pressure for decision-making increases and initial discussion enthusiasm gives way to exhausted compromising.

In such a climate, it is not so easy to maintain the ability to criticize, which is necessary for constructive and mindful decisions. A Time-Out can re-establish the necessary distance and clear mind.

What lies in the hands of everyone at the team level is equally important for each individual. In an interview. M.H. shares that he deliberately blocks time in his calendar to avoid becoming "driven". Over the years, he has learned to give himself the freedom to cancel appointments and, at times, to be available only to a small circle: "I want to take the time to really delve into some things."

---

[4] Brown, Brenè: Dare to lead, London 2018, p. 68.

Decisions take time. Especially in complex and driven times, it is all the more important to develop a sense for moments of distance, breaks, and reflections to cultivate sustainable and conscious decision-making.

Even within the team, it is useful to reflect on which decision rhythms work well. One possibility, for example, is to record an initial impulsive gut decision, and then gain distance to meet again and delve into the analytical perspective. The rhythm between individual and internal team dialogue can change depending on the decision at hand.

Take your time as a team to structure the decision-making process. Perhaps it will help you to appoint someone to lead, moderate, and collect the (interim) results.

Embodiment

In coaching contexts, I increasingly involve the intuitive body feeling in decision-making processes. It is often astonishing how clear the signals are when time and space is given to physically feel into different options.

For example, if an either-or decision needs to be taken, spaces can be used to position the decision options in them. Not without reason is there often talk of sitting "between the chairs". Representing several options available, chairs can be placed at different positions in the room. In addition, objects and written keywords help to visualize and make the options tangible. In mindfulness and meditation practice, the phrase "sit with it" often falls in the face of problems or decisions. The idea behind it is not to continue avoiding the decision-making process, but to deal with the options in a concentrated manner and to fully feel into the consequences. Whether in the lotus position or sitting on a chair—the cognitive change of perspective is often easier when the body is involved in decision-making processes.

This practice is compatible with the psychological or sociological principle of embodiment. In each case, the term responds to cognitivist tendencies of the sciences, which prefer an (over-) emphasis on the mental exploration of social and psychological processes. Even in decision-making, it is often assumed that pure mental investigation points the way. However, cognition is always connected with the body and as much as we would sometimes like to assume purely analytical decision-making ability—the body, our feelings and our experiences are always part of our decision-making patterns. And we can learn a lot from these parts. How often do all rational arguments speak for one direction while the body resists and intuitively wants to take a completely different path?

Decisions that recognize the intelligence and sensitivity of the body do not resist its signals, but integrate them into the process. This does not mean acting headlessly and trusting exclusively in gut feeling.

M. H. also tells that, when hiring new employees, he makes sure that they use their "heart, stomach, and head" and are capable of holistic decisions and perspectives. In our conversation, he shares that for him personally and for his leadership style, the balance between all three is important.

As with any form of balance, this style never be static, but a process in itself, a circling around the center.

Turning to the heart at all, opening it, listening to its signals and involving it in leadership practice takes courage. Brené Brown calls this holistic integration of thinking, feeling, and behavior *wholeheartedness.*[5] It requires the courage to be vulnerable and trusting teams- to make decisions on this basis.

Mindfulness practices can help to hold space for the different perspectives on a problem and to untangle the decision-making process. Not always is there real time pressure due to external circumstances, but it manifests itself as an internal feeling. Especially with difficult decisions, the impulse can arise to make them quickly in order to get rid of them. Especially then, it is helpful to change perspective and view the decision from a larger time span and relation.

The decision pressure builds up when zooming into it until the A- or B- option condenses into an existential basic question.

If the process is reversed and zoomed out from the concrete situation, a deep relaxation can occur, which is important for sustainable decision-making.

Reflection questions

1. What does the decision look like from a bird's eye view?
2. What if there was no "deadline" for the decision?
3. What do you need, what do you all need, to let the pressure subside for a moment?

Focusing on the breath can also be very helpful in making difficult decisions. On the one hand, deep breathing helps for reaching a more relaxed state and on the other hand, it helps for perceiving and interpreting the signals of the body. The breath is a sensitive instrument that subtly reveals whether a decision appears to be the right one. Again, this does not replace weighing up arguments or the tried and tested pro-con list, but it can usefully complement the more mind-focused techniques.

Decisions are often strongly linked to the impulse of people pleasing. Wanting to please everyone can result in saying yes to everything, even if a task, for example, does not meet the company's values or the team is already completely overworked.

The question of how easy it is individually or team-based to say no can also be a good starting point for the reflection of decision-making patterns.

Reflection questions

1. How well are your decision-making processes structured?
2. On what principle (competence-, consensus- or role-oriented) do you make decisions?

---

[5] Brown, Brené: Rising Strong, London 2015, p. 274.

3. How well can you say no? Do you say no often enough or perhaps even too often?
4. Do you make decisions more from the heart, the head, or the gut?
5. How much time do you allow for decision-making?
6. And finally (again a question for the covert survey): On a scale of 1-10, how satisfied are you with your decision-making?
7. What do you possibly want to change?

Inspiration

The Duden, following the Latin translations, suggests two meanings of inspiration:

1. Creative idea, thought, sudden realization, enlightening idea that leads someone forward, especially in intellectual activity. Enlightenment, intuition.
2. Inhalation.

While creativity encompasses the entire process of creating, inspiration describes the spark, the spontaneous intuition that stands at its beginning or marks the moment of becoming aware. The definition according to Duden also refers to the enlightening, even illuminating moment that an idea can unfold. Moments when a light sparks and knowledge becomes possible, where one might have been groping in the dark before. The German analogies of *intuition* and also *idea* suggest that a receptive and open attitude is necessary to be inspired. Inspiration usually does not happen "just like that", but is tied to the willingness to open oneself to receiving ideas and to let the spark shine. In a small survey on the question: What inspires you? in my environment, the following answers were repeatedly given: Art, architecture, people, conversations, books, nature, travel, and fashion. But also characteristics were often described, such as: when people go their own way, when people develop new perspectives, but also: courage.

What favors inspiration is as diverse and individual as what it expresses. Inspiration cannot be forced, it has a constitutive moment of unavailability, as is also characteristic for the state of flow or happiness. Anyone who has ever tried desperately to be inspired or to have an idea will know what I mean.

Already here the second dimension of meaning of inspiration begins, whose root word also goes back to breath for a reason. While the German Duden description includes the rather medical consideration of inspiration as inhalation, the Latin *spiritus* encompasses not only the entire breath, but also *soul* and *spirit*. If one starts from inspiration as openness for "ideas", one can ask: From where do

N. Plohr, *Mindful Leadership*, https://doi.org/10.1007/978-3-658-48300-5_23

they come, the ideas, the enlightening thoughts? And how can one be open for them?

Starting with the breath, breathing is a sensitive instrument for our physical and mental state. It shows us whether we are in a relaxed state, whether it can flow freely, the chest is open and deep breaths are possible. Conversely, certain breathing techniques influence our mental and physical well-being. A prolonged exhalation has calming effects, a prolonged inhalation is energizing, the so-called alternate breathing unfolds a balancing effect. Also, unidirectional inhalation through one nostril can either have a calming (left in, right out) or stimulating (right in, left out) effect.

Breathing techniques and inspiration are closely related and a state of openness, receptivity, and relaxation can be promoted through the breath. Inspiration usually does not occur when we are stressed or overwhelmed, but rather when we have resources available and are relaxed at the same time.

Although inspiration cannot be artificially generated, there are circumstances that promote it and others that tend to prevent it. Especially in teams, it is not always easy to consider the individual rhythms and settings in which inspiration is possible. Self-reflection and initiative are again required to apply the practices of Inner Leadership and to provide the most individually inspiring setting within the given framework.

At the team and company level, the question arises under which overarching vision the inspiration and motivation of the employees can be maintained. Simon Sinek developed the model of the Golden Circle for this approach.[1] He suggests that companies first develop and formulate a why that goes beyond the service offered or the product to be sold.[2] The way to a company's why is paved by the consistent question of what lies deep behind the company's offer. Apple, for example, does not just sell digital devices, but follows the slogan: *We believe in thinking differently.*[3]

This basic idea or *purpose* initially points far beyond laptops and smartphones. The why exists independently of and at the same time intertwined with the product that is bought in the store. At the same time, the why points the way for the how and the what. From the inside out, the Golden Circle follows the logic of a gradual concretization of an initially quite abstract idea or direction. The why often integrates the original idea or the founding story from which the company takes its starting point. According to Sinek, the why is the basis of all subsequent innovations, ideas, and changes of direction.

The why is, so to speak, the original spark of a company, which ideally repeatedly stimulates it to translate it into other forms of how and what.

For a 'why' to contribute to inspiration and innovation in the long term, it must be formulated as openly as specific. Inspiration needs a framework, a reference

[1] Sinek, Simon: Start with Why, New York 2009, p. 37 ff.

[2] Ibid.

[3] Ibid. p. 41.

point, and certain structures of continuity. Ideas also need a certain framework, while free fall remains groundless.

Similar to the fascination with the *Purpose*, I see the risk that the 'why' can also become a stress factor. My students repeatedly share with me and the group how difficult it is for them to formulate their *Purpose*. The *Purpose pressure* is increasingly noticeable not only among individuals but also among companies.

A colleague recently said with a wink: "Nobody sells ice cream anymore, there are only life-changing, world-improving, sustainable, biodegradable basil-lemon-ginger specialties."

I think, he has a point there. Also a student of mine, who soberly and clearly stated in one of my seminars: "Purpose is a privilege."

When time, space, and financial resources are available, the question of Purpose can more easily unfold. If basic needs are not met, the overarching search for the 'why' quickly gives way to the most fundamental existential questions.

If sufficient resources are available, reflection can take place at both the individual and corporate level:

- Do we need a 'why' at this point in time? Can we even formulate it now, or is it too early?
- What inclusion and exclusion processes are associated with the formulation of the 'why'? Is it a 'why' that gives us enough space and freedom for inspiration?

The 'why' is often associated with the level of doing, less with being. A *Purpose* can also be expressed in a specific quality or characteristic that is not necessarily associated with a particular professional field, but communicates itself beyond doing, more in the being. The Purpose pressure increases when it becomes a compulsion for decision and meaningfulness. The feeling that can arise is not being allowed to do *just* a job anymore, but having to find fulfillment and existential meaning in it.

So it becomes clear: A 'why' can be a source of inspiration, but it can also lead to a tipping point where the desire for innovation and wealth of ideas turn into stress. The idea that a 'why' is needed to start at all is not particularly encouraging. Therefore, the 'why' is a concept that must be discussed and tested for suitability within the team before it is used. Nevertheless, it opens up spaces for reflection to become aware of one's own tasks and qualities at a meta-level and to detach them from the product or the specific service. In the best case, the 'why' paves the way for a sense of meaningfulness and also provides a starting point for a wealth of ideas.

According to Simon Sinek, the 'why' is oriented towards the past, it can contain a founding story or an original value that runs through the company's history. This approach is complemented by the so-called *Just Cause,* which points a direction for the future and drafts a vision that goes beyond the company or the individual project. Simon Sinek writes: "A Just Cause [...] describes the world we hope to live in and will commit to help build."[4] Even if this project seems ambitious, it can be very inspiring to commit to a big idea and follow a vision that may seem utopian at first glance. In many of my conversations with executives, but also professors, the sentence kept coming up: "Well, actually I just wanted to do it better than I experienced it myself..." This would already be a Just Cause, which, however, becomes more concrete when it not only distinguishes itself from the given, but also creates its own image of a positive future for the company or the institution.

Starting from the 'why' (if there is one):

- Do you have a Just Cause?
- A clear direction? A vision, an overarching goal?

In an interview with Brené Brown, Simon Sinek describes how many companies lost their goal orientation due to the COVID-19 pandemic.[5] Many executives felt as if they were searching for the way in the fog, struggling with ever-changing uncertainties by regulating not only their own, but also the team's internal uncertainty. Both the Just Cause and the 'why' can contribute at a meta-level to continuity and orientation being given despite adverse circumstances. A certain degree of security is beneficial to inspiration and the curiosity that comes with it.

This applies not only to corporate structures but also at the individual level. Often, good ideas, inspiring sparks find their way to us when we create a calm, secure surrounding for ourselves in which we can relax. This starts sometimes by turning to the present moment and letting silence settle in.

In particular, as a response to loud, rather extroverted, lively conversations and environments that stimulate the mind and body, silence is an important counterpart. When the external impressions are allowed to subside and not just remain on the surface, they lead to the emergence of personal impulses and ideas finding their way into consciousness.

Constant noise and sensory overload are not conducive to inspiration, but rather lead to one's own ideas being buried or overlooked.

Mindfulness helps to find the balance between stimulating input and silence, and also to learn to distinguish between good ideas and the never stopping stream of thoughts. Maintaining distance from one's own thoughts allows them to be sifted, categorized, but also to let them flow. If thoughts do not flow and inspiration stalls, it can help, following the original meaning of the word, to consciously focus on the breath and its natural flow. Breathing and thinking are intertwined, and even though the dictionary refers to inspiration as a mental activity, it is always anchored at the physical level.

---

[4] Sinek, Simon: The infinite Game, USA 2019, p. 33.

[5] Podcast: Dare to Lead by Brené Brown: Episode Brené with Simon Sinek on Developing an Infinite Mindset, 18.01.2021, last accessed: 28.06.2022.

Exercises

1. Finding silence
   Take a few deep breaths and let the impressions of the recent past subside. Perhaps specific situations come to mind, images, people, encounters, perhaps also feelings. Notice what appears before your inner eye, but do not hold on to it. Let your thoughts pass. Arrive in the observer position. You are not your thoughts. Now start to notice your reactions to the images you see. Where does your body start to tingle, when do you feel joy, when does something inside you contract? Consciously direct your attention to the joyful, tingling moments. Experience the quality, the specific energy of these images. Continue to stay in the observer position. What inspires you about the selected moments?
2. Enthusiasm Briefing
   Enthusiasm and inspiration are closely related. Both are somewhat "contagious", they easily transfer within groups that maintain a familiar and open interaction with each other. Beyond the content, it can have an enormously stimulating effect when people share their ability to be enthusiastic. Even a lecture on a topic that is not catching your attention, can ignite the spark of enthusiasm, if the speaker is willing and able to share and embody fascination. Often in teams that frequently present ideas internally, over time the content takes precedence over the form and a factual processing of facts replaces the inspiring spark. The Enthusiasm Briefing counteracts this. Make it your task to let your team colleagues participate in your own enthusiasm. What fascinates you about the idea you want to present? What was the original impulse? What makes you feeling excited about it? Share your enthusiasm without sinking into blind euphoria and create moments of mutual inspiration.

Beginners Mind

The so-called Beginner's Mind also contributes to the ability to be inspired. In companies, often a certain routine develops over time, which can easily switch to automatism. Even in private life, it quickly happens that the tiny, everyday wonders give way to a feeling of self-evidence. In the Zen Buddhist tradition, the Beginner's Mind is the fresh, open, unbiased turning towards the present, which allows us to stay aware and curious for the diversity of life. Instead of constantly needing to acquire something new, the familiar is repeatedly rediscovered with a sense of astonishment. Shunruy Suzuki describes this with the following words: "In the beginner's mind there are many possibilities, in the expert's mind there are a few."[1]

A Beginner's Mindset does not assume to possess the truth or to form a final judgment about the present. Instead, one's own tendencies to judge are observed without identifying with them.

Especially in teams that have been working together for a long time, as well as in companies with established structures and traditions, it can happen that the desire for innovation gives way to the tried and true "but we've always done it this way". New employees are then primarily confronted with the task of fitting into these structures. Their often justified questions and criticisms, which could point out important blind spots in a company and initiate change, are frequently capped with a call for adaptation.

New team members ideally embody the Beginner's Mindset. They look at their new work environment with fresh eyes, have not yet learned any fixed rules about what can and cannot be said, thought, and expressed. This phase of "onboarding" brings with it vulnerability and effort, but is also an opportunity to look at the company again with curiosity and a sense of beginning. Instead of confronting the onboarding process directly with established rules and structures, one possibility

[1] Suzuki, Shunruy: Zen Mind, Beginner's Mind, Colorado 2020, p. 2.

N. Plohr, *Mindful Leadership*, https://doi.org/10.1007/978-3-658-48300-5_24

to stimulate the Beginner's Mind would be to first observe and share impressions. This way, newcomers do not feel like additional baggage, but as a source of fresh perspectives and ideas.

Even as a long-term employee or executive, the Beginner's Mindset offers valuable perspectives. As the introductory quote from Shunruy Suzuki implies, the Beginner's Mind opens up a multitude of paths and possibilities, while expertise tends to refer to what has already been learned and thus runs the risk of narrowing one's own view.

The work of sociologists also follows the principle of the Beginner's Mind when they conduct research with the aim of being as prejudice-free as possible. Ideally, they observe as freshly and openly as possible, only to begin the theoretical coding of the collected material afterwards. This is related to mindfulness practice, because in (auto-)ethnography, but also in interview settings, it is important to perceive and name one's own prejudices and assumptions as such, in order to expose and reflect as many of one's own conditions and blind spots as possible. Self-reflection and self-knowledge are indispensable for reflecting on the observed field and its dynamics.

The more sociologists are personally involved in the field to be observed, the more difficult it is often to maintain a Beginner's Mindset. But even in uncovering the differences between the experienced, trained perspective and the struggle of beginning, valuable insights can occur. "The beginner's mind is the mind of compassion"[2] , writes Shunryu Suzuki. Empathy is trained by remembering the beginner's mind and also the hurdles and fears associated with the insecure steps into the unknown of a new beginning.

In my coaching sessions with companies and especially with executives, I often feel that it is difficult to put oneself in the shoes of the beginner. Especially when the challenges on one's own path have already been overcome successfully and forgotten or suppressed on the way to the top. From the perspective of the CEO, it is of course no problem to solve the tasks of an intern. For a professor the struggles with a first research paper may seem exaggerated. The art of the Beginner's Mind liess in reclaiming the struggle, the sense of wonder, the questioning and willingness to try. It involves cultivating compassion for the individual paths of others while also recognizing the value of a fresh perspective on established structures.

This awareness offers the opportunity to challenge and reset the existing mindset, which is established on an individual level and continues in the structures of the company.

Where, perhaps, has your team lost the joy of curiosity and marveling? How can the Beginner's Mindset be re-awakened?

Newcomers can offer fres impulses by entering the company from the outside, but shifts inperspective are equally possible from within. Tap into the power of imagination to cultivate the Beginner's Mindset: What if this were your very first

[2] Suzuki, Shunruy: Zen Mind, Beginner's Mind, Colorado 2020, p. 2. or Ibid.

meeting? What would you do, if you were preparing for your first customer interaction? What if you were presenting your first idea?

And for all the meaning that lies in clear processes and routines: Where might they be rethought, restructured, constructively disrupted or opened up?

On a meta-level, Thich Nath Hanh writes: "All is a miracle."[3] By "miracles," he does not refer to supernatural or superhuman events, but to the everyday willingness to remain aware of the miracle of being alive. "People usually consider walking on water or in thin air a miracle. But I think the real miracle is not to walk either on water or in thin air, but to walk on earth."[4]

This often begins with becoming aware of one's own body, breath, and the everyday taken-for-granted: "If you breathe in mindfully, you touch the miracle of being alive."[5], says Thich Nath Hanh.

This conscious turning towards one's own body is also found in sociology, when, for example, Loic Wacquant calls in his research to integrate the researcher's body as an instrument of emotional awareness into the observations.[6]

This can also be applied in leadership contexts. The body often sends clear signals when, for example, communication processes go awry or negotiations develop in an unfavorable direction. It also signals when ideas trigger a tingling sensation or put every cell into a state of excitement. The beginner's mindset is aware of these signals and not paralyzed by the familiar. Especially in times of change, a fundamental openness for the present moment is helpful. If the beginner's mind is practiced, even when everything is running *according to routine*, the ability to respond to unpredictability with flexibility and creativity is simultaneously trained. Shunruy Suzuki writes: "It is the readiness of the mind that is wisdom."[7]

This does not mean responding to new challenges with outdated concepts, but rather acting in tune with the situation at hand. In the spirit of the Beginner's mind, the mind is truly *ready*, when it remains open, as free from prejudice as possible, and capable of embracing a fresh view of the here and now.

What sounds simple is often not so easy to implement in practice. A first step toward cultivating a beginner's mind can be taken by becoming aware of one's predispositions and ingrained patterns. For instance, M. H. describes that many potential employees enter the application process with high expectations and firmly held ideas. If these attitudes are so rigid that they obscure a clear view of the company or preemptively reject the unfamiliar, the openness essential to a beginner's mind is lost.

---

[3] Thich Nath Hanh: The Miracle of Mindfulness, Rider 2008, p. 12.

[4] Ibid.

[5] Wacquant, Loic: *For a Sociology of Flesh and Blood*, in: sub/urban, Journal for Critical Urban Research, Volume 2, Issue 3, 2014.

[6] Ibid.

[7] Suzuki, Shunruy: Zen Mind, Beginners Mind, Colorado 2020, p. 103.

Regardless of one's position in a company, it is valuable to examine one's own assumptions and perceived certainties—and to dare to take the perspective of a new beginning.

The beginner's mind is also woven into the cultivation of Mindful Leadership practices. While guides, courses, and workshops on the subject are increasingly abundant and competing for attention, the deeper question remains largely unsolved: How can mindfulness be genuinely integrated into the practice of leadership?.

And so, this book ultimately offers more questions than answers. It sees itself not as source of final definitions or fixed conclusion, but as an invitation- to reflect, engage, and to draw inspiration for both theory and practice.

I understand Mindful Leadership as a broad, evolving concept- both a framework and a lived practice that continuously respond to current needs and to the increasingly urgent call for change. At the same time it returns us to essential human questions and challenges, such as:

- How do we stay present?
- How do we navigate uncertainty and change?
- How do we meet one another?
- How can collaboration become co-creation?
- How do we open ourselves to greater diversity?
- How can we build companies that are truly sustainable?

The beginner's mind runs through all these questions, reminding us that no final answers or ready-made action templates exist. Rather than relying on and holding onto outdated concepts, now is the time for curiosity, openness, and change.

And so, I would like to conclude this final chapter once again with a few reflection questions and a practical exercise. My hope is, that they will find their way beyond theory and into everyday (corporate) life.

Reflection questions

1. When was the last time you did something for the first time?
2. When did you as a team last dare to try something new?
3. What assumptions do you hold about your company, your team, or even about yourselves?
4. In what ways might those assumptions be limiting you?
5. How do you welcome and support new arrivals?
6. Are there already techniques, tools, formats or types of conversations, in which the beginner's mindset is encouraged?
7. How do you help newcomers feel safe when it comes to making mistakes?
8. How much of a beginner's mind is embodied by your team?
9. And how much of a beginner's mind do you embody?

Exercise 'Beginner's Mind

Actively shift into a beginner's mindset. Walk through a typical (work) day as if it were your first. Pay close attention to your surroundings, focus on your senses. What do you see, what do you hear, what do you feel? What is the atmosphere of the rooms you move through? What is the lighting like? How does the floor feel beneath your feet?

How do people interact with you? How do you greet one another? What emotions are reflected in their faces?

Become aware of your own routines. Which moments of the day do you usually go through on autopilot?

Bring mindfull attention to these moments. Stay present. Notice them. Let your gaze switch between details and the big picture, zoom into small differences , then zoom back out to the balcony perspective. Stay curious and relaxed at the same time. Allow yourself to be surprised by the ordinary. Look closely. Engage fully. Stay open.

Mindset and Reset

Catch yourself during the day when judgements or preconceptions arise. Write them down. Become aware of your mindset, your thought patterns. How do you evaluate situations, encounters and tasks? Are your assessments grounded in, the present moment, or shaped by past experiences? Is a re-evaluation possible? A change of perspective?

Ask yourself: What if I were experiencing this moment for the first time today? Start all over again ☺.

Conclusion

At the beginning of this book were stood premises, two hypotheses. First: Every person is a leader. And second: The way we lead ourselves is the way we lead others.

The first hypothesis was not confirmed by my interview partners. In every conversation, it was emphasized that leadership requires courage, decisiveness, and empathy. Most importantly, it was repeatedly emphasized that leadership begins with a conscious decision—to step into it, and to take on the responsibility that comes with it. This increased responsibility was understood primarily as a responsibility for others, beyond oneself. However, as one executive pointed out, this responsibility can also be directed toward a specific topic or area of expertise.

This implies the following: Even if employees are not in formal leadership positions, those who contribute their own ideas and take responsibility for topics and tasks demonstrate leadership qualities. Conversely, simply holding a leadership title is by no means a guarantee for actual leadership competence.

It was striking how quickly-especially executives in leadership positions-dismissed my admittedly somewhat provocative thesis. My argument that every person leads a life and defines themselves through that life, was considered insufficient in every case. Self-responsibility was assumed, but the willingness to be make an impact beyond one's own life was considered essential to leadership. Yet based on my observations throughout this book project, as well as in workshops and trainings with companies, in coaching settings, and in personal conversations, the importance of self-responsibility is often underestimated and taken for granted.

Leading oneself in complex and challenging times, taking responsibility one's inner life, thought patterns and emotional responses , is a continuous process that is never completed or finally resolved. In the sense of Thich Nhat Hanh's concept of Interbeing, our self-leadership is influenced by multifaceted external aspects. At the same time, we externalize much of what occupies us internally. Inside and outside, outside and inside—they are in a constant interplay, continuously intertwined and both demand our presence.

This brings me to the second thesis from which this book has taken its starting point: The way we lead ourselves is the way we lead others. Throughout the of this book project, it has once again became clear how important regular self-reflection

N. Plohr, *Mindful Leadership*, https://doi.org/10.1007/978-3-658-48300-5

is—both in relation to others people and for personal growth. This begins with the inner dialogue, the inner with the inner storytellers and critics, continues with the ability to develop empathy and decision-making, and it finds provisional closure with the Beginner's Mind, which continually redefines the task of leadership anew. There is no way around self-responsibility and the inner leadership work.

At the same time, I would like to expand the second thesis with observations that have emerged particularly through exploring topics such as error culture, recognition, and empathy.

The inner and outer are not always in sync. Sometimes the pattern is reversed. For example, a lack of self-empathy may be accompanied by excessive empathy for others, or an inner hunger for recognition might manifest as a withholding praise from others. There is always a correlation between the internal and external, but they do not always mirror one another directly.

To trace these specific connections and engage more deeply with them requires attention and courage to face one's own patterns. Mindfulness resides precisely in the combination of presence, attention, and reflective awareness.

For me, Mindful Leadership means exactly this: maintaining balance between the internal and external, being and staying present, and holding space for oneself and others. Beyond that, it means embracing the interconnectedness of interbeing as connection between ourselves, our organizations and goals, and the broader whole. It is a practice, not a dogma, not a raised finger, one that is individually shaped and capable of holding space for a diversity of themes and questions. I have explored a few of these in this book and offered them as invitations for further reflections.

"The word mindfulness can sometimes get on my nerves [...]"[1] writes Brené Brown, and I get the sense that she is not alone in this.

Like so many buzzwords, mindfulness also runs the risk of exhausting itself, its meaning diluted by overuse. But perhaps what becomes irritating about mindfulness is not jus the word, but the present itself, which we not always be willing or ready to meet with full awareness. Especially in times like these, when the multifaceted challenges become so dense and converge with a growing sense of urgency.

And yet, to enable change and create new possibilities, we cannot bypass the present. And this brings us full circle to what Mindfulness truly means and what it offers as a practice: The art of being present, of recognizing the here and now in all its complexity, and of continually asking:

How present, how conscious, and how connected am I right now?

[1]Brown, Brené: Dare to lead, London 2018, p. 149.

References

Breidenbach, Joana/Rollow, Bettina: New Work needs Inner Work, München 2019.
Bröckling, Ulrich: Das unternehmerische Selbst, Berlin 2007.
Brown Brené: Braving the Wilderness, New York 2017.
Brown, Brené: Atlas of the heart, New York 2021.
Brown, Brenè: Dare to lead, London 2018.
Brown, Brené: Rising Strong, London 2015.
Clear, James: Atomic Habits. London 2018.
Csikszentmihalyi, Mihaly: Flow und Kreativität, Stuttgart 1997.
Csikszentmihalyi, Mihaly: Flow. Das Geheimnis des Glücks, Stuttgart 1992.
Endriss, Lilo: Fahrplan für den Flow, Wiesbaden 2019.
Esther und Johannes Narbeshuber: Mindful Leader. Wie wir die Führung für unser Leben in die Hand nehmen und uns Gelassenheit zum Erfolg führt, München 2019.
Foucault, Michel: Was ist Kritik? Berlin 1992.
Funke, Joachim: Zur Psychologie der Kreativität, in: Dresler/Baudsen: Kreativität. Beiträge aus den Natur- und Geisteswissenschaften, Stuttgart 2008.
Gilbert, Elizabeth: Big Magic, New York 2015.
Gonzalez, Maria: Mindful Leaderhsip. The 9 ways to self awareness, transforming yourself and inspiring others, Ontario 2012.
Jain, Shaminin: Healing ourselves: Biofield science and the future of health, Colorado 2021.
Janice Marturano: Mindful Leadership. Ein Weg zu achtsamer Führungskompetenz, Freiburg 2015.
Kabat-Zinn, Jon: Gesund durch Meditation, München 2013.
Lessenich, Stefan: Neben uns die Sintflut, München 2016, S. 196, zit. nach: Göpel, Maja: unsere Welt neu denken. Eine Einladung, Berlin 2020.
Lorelei Kopp: Mindful Leadership: Tools und Methoden für achtsames Führen in turbulenten Zeiten, Graz 2021.
McLuhan, Marshall, Powers, Bruce R.: The Global Village. Transformation in World Life and Media in the 21st Century, Oxford 1989.
Michael Carroll: The Mindful Leader, Colorado 2007.
Pavitt, Neil: Brainhack: Tips and Tricks to unleash your brain's full potential, UK/Cornwall 2016.
Plohr, Nikola: Was ist Selftracking? Eine Autoethnografie des vermessenen Selbst, Bielefeld 2021.
Rosa, Hartmut: Resonanz. Eine Soziologie der Weltbeziehung, Berlin 2016.
Rosendorfer, Herbert: Briefe in die chinesische Vergangenheit, München 1986.
Schatzki, Theodore: Social Practices – A Wittgensteinian Approach to Human Activity and the Social. Cambridge 1996.
Serres, Michel: Erfindet euch neu! Eine Liebeserklärung an die vernetzte Generation, Berlin 2013.

N. Plohr, *Mindful Leadership,* https://doi.org/10.1007/978-3-658-48300-5

Sinek, Simon: Start with Why, New York 2009.
Sinek, Simon: The Infinite Game, USA 2019.
Spreen, Dierk: Upgradekultur. Der Körper in der Enhancement Gesellschaft, Bielefeld 2015.
Stahl, Stefanie: Das Kind in dir muss Heimat finden, München 2015.
Steinem, Gloria: Revolution from Within, Boston/Toronto/London 1992.
Suzuki, Shunruy: Zen Mind, Beginners Mind, Colorado 2020.
Thich Nath Hanh: The Art of living, New York 2017.
Thich Nath Hanh: The miracle of Mindfulness, Rider 2008.
Virilio, Paul: Rasender Stillstand, Berlin 2008.
Wacquant, Loic: Für eine Soziologie aus Fleisch und Blut, in: sub/urban, Zeitschrift für kritische Stadtforschung, Band 2, Heft 3, 2014.

Online Sources:

Davis, Mark H. (1980). A multidimensional approach to individual differences in empathy. JSAS Catalog of Selected Documents in Psychology, vol.10, pp.85ff. Davis, Mark H. (1983). Empathic concern and the muscular dystrophy telethon. Empathy as a multidimensional construct. Personality and Social Psychology Bulletin, vol.9, no. 2, pp.223–229. (Stangl, 2021).
Fernsehformat „Precht", Svenka Faßplöhler im Gespräch: Sensibilisieren wir uns zu Tode, 04.12.2021, https://www.youtube.com/watch?v=OkaNritD8PM, zuletzt aufgerufen: 04.03.2022.
Mindful Journal, Mindful Staff: 10.01.2016, https://www.mindful.org/smartphones-hurt-our-face-to-face-relationships-sherry-turkle/, zuletzt aufgerufen: 19.12.2022.
Stangl, W. (2021). Stichwort: *‚Empathie – Online Lexikon für Psychologie und Pädagogik'*. Online Lexikon für Psychologie und Pädagogik. https://lexikon.stangl.eu/1095/empathie (2021–12–02).
Paech, Niko: Grundzüge einer Postwachstumsökonomie (2009), http://www.postwachstumsoekonomie.de/material/grundzuege/, zuletzt aufgerufen: 27.06.2022.
Persönlichkeitspsychologie und Diagnostik, Universität Zürich: https://www.charakterstaerken.org/VIA_Interpretationshilfe.pdf, zuletzt aufgerufen: 27.06.2022.
Podcast Debbie Millman: Design Matters: Maurice Cherry, 03.08.2020, zuletzt aufgerufen: 27.06.2022.
Podcast von Brené Brown Dare to Lead: Brené with Liz Wiseman on Impact Players, 18.10.2021, zuletzt aufgerufen: 27.06.2022.
Podcast: Dare to Lead von Brené Brown: Episode Brené with Simon Sinek on Developing an Infinite Mindset, 18.01.2021, zuletzt aufgerufen: 28.06.2022.
Podcast: Hotel Matze: Kevin Kühnert- Glaubst du alles, was du sagst, 06.04.2022, zuletzt aufgerufen: 27.06.2022.
Podcast: Nora Jacobs: Creativity x you, Episode 2: Was versteht man überhaupt unter Kreativität? aufgerufen zuletzt via Spotify: 04.03.2022.
Vocer-Institut in Hamburg zum Begriff der „Digitalen Resilienz": https://digitale-resilienz.org/#digitale-resilienz, zuletzt aufgerufen: 19.12.2022.
Wickert, N., Meents, A. Resilienz – Die innere Widerstandskraft. Z Psychodrama Soziom19, 1–5 (2020). https://doi.org/10.1007/s11620-020-00523-7. Zuletzt aufgerufen: 08.02.2022.

The manufacturer's authorised representative in the EU is Springer Nature Customer Service Centre GmbH, Europaplatz 3, 69115 Heidelberg, Germany. If you have any concerns regarding our products, please contact ProductSafety@springernature.com

Printed and bound by CPI Group (UK) Ltd, Croydon, CR0 4YY
30/09/2026
02225606-0019